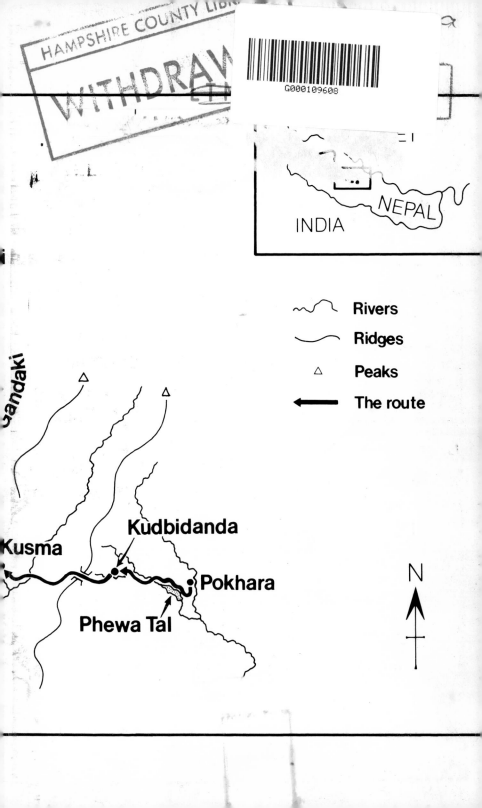

INDIA · NEPAL

Rivers
Ridges
△ Peaks
← The route

Gandaki

Kudbidanda

Kusma

Pokhara

Phewa Tal

N

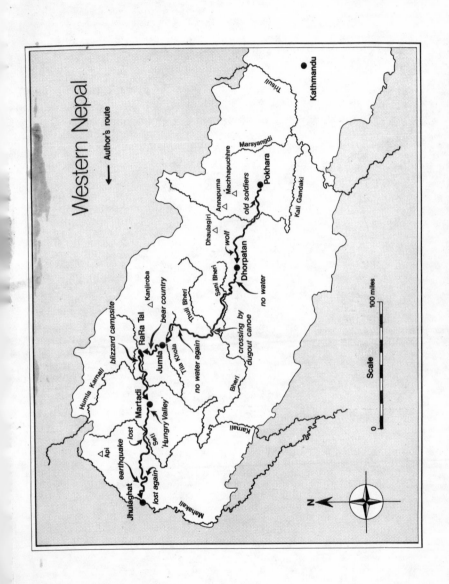

Western Nepal

← Author's route

Kathmandu

Trisuli

Marsyangdi

Annapurna △
Machhapuchhre △
old soldiers
Pokhara

Dhaulagiri △

wolf

Sani Bheri

Dhorpatan

no water

Kanjiroba △
bear country

Thuli Bheri

RaRa Tal

Tila Khola

Jumla

no water again

crossing by
dugout canoe

Humla Karnali

blizzard campsite

Martadi

Bheri

Karnali

'Hungry Valley'

lost

Seti

△ Api

earthquake

Jhulaghat

lost again

Mahakali

N

Scale

0   100 miles

Into Thin Air

By the same author (with Hilary Bradt)

Backpacking in Chile and Argentina

Into Thin Air

JOHN PILKINGTON

London
GEORGE ALLEN & UNWIN
Boston   Sydney

George Allen & Unwin (Publishers) Ltd,
40 Museum Street, London, WC1A 1LU, UK

George Allen & Unwin (Publishers) Ltd,
Park Lane, Hemel Hempstead, Herts HP2 4TE, UK

George Allen & Unwin Australia Pty Ltd,
8 Napier Street, North Sydney, NSW 2060, Australia

George Allen & Unwin with the
Port Nicholson Press
PO Box 11-838 Wellington, New Zealand

First published 1985

ISBN 0 04 910085 8

Set in 11 on 12½ point Sabon by Computape (Pickering) Limited, N. Yorkshire
and printed in Great Britain by Thetford Press Limited, Thetford, Norfolk

Contents

List of Illustrations

Acknowledgements

The story that follows owes much to many people. I should like to thank especially Messrs Blacks of Greenock and J. M. Loveridge of Southampton who generously provided some important items of equipment. Jim Fulton, at that time British Vice-Consul in Kathmandu, extended his services well beyond the call of duty and helped to ease my path in Nepal. Jill Willder made thoughtful suggestions during the writing, and, with Bob Gibbons and Diana Nicoll, helped turn my bedraggled field notes into something like the present book – a task aided by typists Valerie Stenning and Margaret Fuller. I am particularly grateful to Jane Kirk for wordprocessing much of the final manuscript, and to Paul Jones for drawing the line illustrations and maps.

A great many others in Britain, India and Nepal lent helping hands to the journey, always generously and often spontaneously. The contribution they made will, I hope, be appreciated by everyone who reads the book.

'The further one travels, the less it seems one knows.'
Lao Tzu, *Tao Te Ching*

Prologue

Dear Beany,

I wonder if this letter will ever reach you? Looking across the muddy street to the post box I'm going to put it in, I can hardly believe it will. Jumla is the capital of Karnali, one of Nepal's fourteen zones, but if that sounds impressive let me add that it's the most unlikely capital city I've ever seen. Its main street has never known the wheel because the nearest road is at least 200 miles away. The mud and timber buildings have no water supply and no electricity, and most of them are plunged into darkness when the sun goes down because hardly anyone has any candles.

You probably think I'm demented to spend Christmas in a place like this. Well, let me confirm your suspicions by saying that I've struggled for three weeks over the mountains to get here. My idea was to walk from Pokhara across north-west Nepal – a desolate but most interesting part of the country where the landscape is dissected by great rivers and the people follow a subsistence way of life more or less unsullied by the outside world. So my few days in this haven of sophistication are a real treat, and I don't mind at all having to sit on the floor and eat with my fingers. Believe it or not, at the moment I'm sitting at a real table, the only one in Jumla as far as I can see. I've been drinking tea, resting my legs and watching the wrinkled old men across the street. There are a great many of these, and they're all knitting. Brows furrowed in concentration, they are taking their work very seriously and have the air of true professionals. The clatter is deafening.

It's much easier to believe in those biblical Christmas scenes when you're walking through an arid, mountainous landscape like that round here. Flocks of sheep are everywhere, the shepherds in their loincloths and blankets looking as if they're just off to appear in a nativity play. Mangers and cribs are commonplace, and the night sky is so alive with twinkling stars that a bright one in the east would hardly be noticed. Admittedly I haven't yet found an inn that can't manage to squeeze in one more guest, but maybe that's because I'm a foreigner.

People here are mostly Buddhists. They don't believe in Christmas, and their New Year comes in the middle of February, but if they understood what I'm writing I'm sure they would want to join me in wishing you the season's greetings. About a dozen of them are looking over my shoulder and nodding their approval.

All the best,

John

1

A Conversation Over Tea

'When I was very young and the urge to be someplace else was upon me, I was assured by mature people that maturity would cure this itch.'

John Steinbeck, *Travels with Charley*

I put down my scratchy Indian ballpoint. It rolled slowly down the length of the table and nuzzled against the packet of mouldy biscuits that the proprietor of the tea-house had proudly offered me. The biscuits were called 'Everest'. The tea was called Brooke Bond. It was syrupy-sweet and cold.

The crowd that had gathered to watch me write had lost interest after the first half hour and had mostly drifted away to tend their sheep. Six, more resilient than the rest, remained perched on the bench opposite, still grinning, pointing and nudging one another as they had done since I arrived. Because this was Nepal, and the gathering was a social one, they were, of course, all men. Three were Tibetans, their buttery faces and maroon homespun *chubas* or cloaks immediately distinguishing them as people from the north. They had just come in from Mugu with their yaks and a cargo of wool. Another two were Hindus, recognisable by their multicoloured *topis* or skull-caps. The rest of their dapper costume – tight, cream-coloured trousers under a dainty matching skirt – was unmistakably that of the Chhetri caste, and the sacks of red 'Jumla' rice at their feet identified them as farmers from one of the local villages. The sixth in the group was a shy, one-armed

1

boy called Ram. He sat silent and motionless but fixed me with penetrating brown eyes.

The tea-house, its contents and its customers blended perfectly. Everything and everyone was blackened by years of proximity to the smoke that curled up from the juniper fire in the middle of the room, so that it was difficult to tell where

one object or person finished and the next began. As my eyes became used to the dark I started to make out details. A kettle simmered on a clay oven by the fire, its steam opaque in the single shaft of sunlight that pierced down from the 'chimney' – a hole in the roof. An array of intricately decorated Tibetan plates and bowls occupied a shelf along one wall. In pride of place, between the silver-plated salver and the brass teapot, stood a jar of Nescafé. On the shelf below lay a freshly amputated buffalo head, blood still dripping from its severed gullet.

Outside in the mountain sunshine, Jumla's diminutive weekly market was doing its best to bustle. Its half dozen stalls were the greatest hub of commerce in the whole of north-west Nepal, and people came from miles around. Here you could buy anything from magic potions to nail clippers.

Jumla distinguished itself from its lesser neighbours in another way too. It had streetlights. Four to be precise: wooden and set at various angles to the vertical, but nevertheless the municipality's pride and joy. They worked on kerosene, and when there was no kerosene, yak butter. The old men knitting round the one opposite the tea-house had been throwing me surreptitious glances when they thought I wasn't looking. Now the eldest detached himself from the group, hobbled over and sat down beside me. '*Namaste sahib!*' he grinned toothlessly, waving his knitting needle. 'We hear you have come over the mountains from Kathmandu. My friends have asked me to extend cordial greetings and welcome you to Jumla. Please, what is your name, your country, your business?'

I fumbled for words. Nepali wasn't my strong point. Name, country, age, mother's and father's names and ages and the price of my boots I had been asked dozens of times. But *business*? What business could an English town planner possibly have in this remote part of a small kingdom in the Himalaya?

The 'business' had begun a year previously when my employers – a county council in the south of England – had given me the opportunity to take six months' unpaid leave to go travelling and writing. I had done some travelling already in Africa, Latin America and Alaska, but had never been east. Now I had the chance to broaden my experiences further: to visit some of the highest mountains in the world and at the same time meet people who, it was said, had found a way of life more balanced than our own.

It was natural, therefore, that my interest should focus on Nepal. The Nepalese derived their outlook from a remarkable combination of Taoist, Confucian and Buddhist influences from China and Tibet together with Hindu elements from their southerly neighbour India. With this unusual blending of beliefs they had developed a reputation for remaining calm and placid, whatever hardships might come their way.

My understanding of the religions of the East, like that of many Westerners, was limited to a few conversations and a superficial acquaintance with basic texts such as the *Ramayana* and the *I Ching*. I had learned just enough to realise that they had a great deal in common. Hindus, for example, strive to unite their *aatmaa* or innermost soul with *brahma*, the spiritual medium in which we all live and which gives us our *dharma* or duty in life. In a surprisingly similar way Buddhists seek enlightenment through following the Eightfold Path towards Nirvana. Meditation and yoga play a fundamental part in the lives of Hindus and Buddhists alike, as indeed they do for many followers of the Tao. The spiritual discipline which is almost a defining characteristic of these religions (and which is so often missing from those in the West) would, I was sure, meet its greatest challenge in the adversities confronting the peasant farmers of the highest and most rugged mountains in the world.

Atlases showed Nepal almost obliterated by that close hatching they use to indicate rough terrain. This notation was particularly evident in the north-east (around Mount Everest) and the north-west. The fact that I could find almost no other information about the north-west of the country convinced me that that was where I should go.

I toyed with the trip for ages. I sought out everything that had been written about north-west Nepal (which wasn't much). I discussed it with anyone who would listen. Even the more detailed maps showed no roads of any kind in that part of the country, so I would have to go on foot. For much of the time I would need to be self-sufficient, especially as the weather in the mountains would be anybody's guess; the only thing I could discover about it was that it was cold. One aspect particularly bothered me. I had come back from the Andes three years previously, laden with photographs of grand mountains and tales of exciting adventures which I had hawked round my friends in the flimsy pretence that I just wanted to share my experiences. I had burrowed away writing articles; I had even helped write a book. Actually, as everyone who has been on a long journey knows, I was simply purveying a fantasy. Robyn Davidson put it best after she had crossed the Western Australian desert with four camels.

They were gorgeous photos, no complaints there, but who was that *Vogue* model tripping romantically along roads with a bunch of camels behind her, hair lifted delicately by sylvan breezes and turned into a golden halo by the back-lighting. Who the hell was she? Never let it be said that the camera does not lie. It lies like a pig in mud. It captures the projections of whoever happens to be using it, never the truth.

If all I intended to do now was fuel the fantasy of Nepal by capturing it on film and in writing, I might as well forget it. The country was having enough trouble coping with its torrents of fantasy-seekers already, without being turned into a museum of the imagination by people like me.

But of all these conflicting intuitions the strongest had said go. No matter if what I found there was fact or fantasy; I would have to judge for myself. There could not, I thought, be many places as difficult to discover anything definite about as north-west Nepal. Maybe I could help fill the gap. With this innocent sense of purpose I posted my proposal for a book to nineteen well-known publishers. Over the next few weeks I received nineteen polite rejections.

Rotten luck? Or a rotten proposal? A friend in publishing gently persuaded me that to the people on the receiving end it must have looked a pretty rotten proposal. Possibly the thirtieth rotten proposal that day. At first I argued; after all, it had taken me a whole week to write. Eventually, however, I agreed that she was probably right. I threw away my nineteen wax images and sat down to write it properly. This time I tried some different publishers, and two months later, just when I had finally given up, I received an invitation from one to come and talk about it. It hardly seemed possible. It was cartwheels round the lawn. It was dinner with champagne. It was hope.

A week later I was sitting with the editorial director in a tiny book-lined office off Bloomsbury Square, expatiating about routes, schedules, dangers and photographic possibilities like a hardened explorer. He politely heard me out, then equally politely grilled me about some of the more obviously improvised details. After an hour he made up his mind. I had convinced him. Whatever the consequences he would support me. For the first time I allowed myself to believe that the trip might actually happen. I skipped down Tottenham Court Road, grinning insanely at the shoppers, treading air.

I started making lists of things to take, arrangements to make, people to see, letters to write, jobs to do. I was amazed at how long the lists were. They covered pages. A friend suggested I should take a Sony Walkman. Another gave me a bottle of whisky to carry. Yet another presented me with a pot-pourri and an introduction to the Maharaja of Gwalior. I broached the question of unpaid leave with my employers, and we agreed that it would suit the ratepayers quite well if I disappeared for the winter, which would fit in with project work in the office. I wrote a pleading letter to the Nepalese Ministry of Home Affairs asking if they would grant me an extended visa for this period, but got no reply. Bother. I would have to try to arrange this when I arrived. Next I had to find some companies willing to sponsor me for the equipment and film I would need. More pleading letters. Medicines would be important, although I knew from past experience that I would probably end up giving most of them away. Somehow I had to find out which ones I would be most likely to need, either for myself or for the assorted ailments I would be bound to find afflicting other travellers along the way.

These practical problems and anxieties dominated my last few days in England. They preoccupied me through my farewell party; they infiltrated the tearful goodbyes, the hugs and kisses and the see-you-next-years. And they were still on my mind as I stepped on to the Ariana Afghan DC-10, bound for Kabul and Delhi.

2

Approach

'Never go abroad, it's a dreadful place.'
Earl of Cadogan

I sat on the tarmac at Kabul airport and gave the fruit fly on
my knee a closer inspection. It was an emaciated specimen –
half the size of British ones, and hungry looking. I tried to swat
it and missed. Half a dozen rodent faces peeked nervously
from under a chapati stall nearby, sized me up as harmless,
and emerged one by one followed by skinny bodies and
spindly tails. They snuffled in the dirt around my feet, stopping occasionally to chomp on any scrap that looked as if it
might contain a crumb of gritty food.

Kabul was plagued by vermin, dust and very young Russian
soldiers toting guns. In spite of these irritations, however, the
Afghans around the airport seemed genuinely cheerful. People
had waved as the DC-10 taxied in among the Sukhoi fighter
planes and Hind helicopters – each machine parked neatly
with its armaments stacked alongside. Smiles were everywhere; a carnival atmosphere was in the air. With all this
military paraphernalia set against the dusty backdrop of
Kabul's gentle surrounding hills, the scene looked like a
sepia-tinted version of the Farnborough Air Show.

My glimpse of Afghanistan – taken under strict security and
limited to the confines of the airport – revealed a strange
mixture of sparkle and despair. It was evident from their faces
that Afghans enjoyed life. All around me eyes twinkled from
behind layers of shawl. But the Soviet presence was heavy and
oppressive, and in this atmosphere people clearly had difficulty in getting on with day-to-day things. I made a spirited

8

attempt to get into Kabul itself during my few hours there, if only for a cup of tea, but was told firmly that visas for such excursions were not available. 'It ees nat verry eenteresting,' said the Russian official in a perfect caricature of himself. Anyway, he pointed out, my plane was just about to leave.

So it did (two hours later) and as we approached Delhi I felt a tightening in my stomach. This was it – the East. The half of the world that gave us silk, spices, paper, and some radical alternative ideas about medicine and philosophy – not to mention tigers and tea. Also, in the case of India, the part of the world where poverty reaches its ultimate, unbelievable extreme. Perhaps I was expecting all these things to slap me in the face immediately, but if so I was disappointed. My arrival was cushioned by the magnificent and unexpected hospitality of the Indian Mountaineering Foundation.

From its headquarters in New Delhi the IMF has organised several of the greatest Himalayan expeditions of recent years, and has helped and nursed hundreds more. I was lucky enough to have an introduction to the president, Harish Sarin. I phoned him from the airport. Over a crackly line Mrs Sarin told me that her husband was unfortunately out playing tennis, but I should make my way to the Foundation's hostel for mountaineers in Anand Niketan and he would meet me there. Her step-by-step directions were hopelessly lost among the crackles. I jotted down what I thought she said, stepped out of the phone booth and inquired tentatively for a taxi. I had forgotten that this was India. Within seconds a hundred taxi drivers fell upon me.

One of the throng finally enticed me into his cab by feigning convincingly that he knew where the IMF was. 'I am telling you, I have taken many fine mountaineers to this place. Yes, it is to be found just off Benito Juarez Road, quite close to here. You will see. Now, if you would be so kind as to step this way, my car awaits you. Yes, it is right here. No, there is no meter. I charge you only forty rupees because you are a visitor. Please.'

When you have just arrived in a country, new to its ways and unsure of the value of money, you've got to face the fact that somewhere along the line you're going to be fleeced. If you choose to arrive at an international airport, tired, hot and jetlagged, you can expect to be ripped off on a grand scale. Of course, I should have bargained, checked the buses, walked round the corner. Instead I sank into the tattered back seat of the cab, breathed in the aroma of stale curry which hung around it like a balloon, and dozed gratefully as we chugged around on three cylinders, looking for the phantom hostel for mountaineers. After an hour and a half we found it, and a concerned Mr Sarin told me that I should have paid no more then ten rupees for the journey. 'But let the matter rest. Welcome to India! I have reserved you a bed. Now, if you would accompany me to the dining room . . .' I followed him towards another aroma, this time fresh. I had arrived right on the dot of suppertime.

Seated at the table were two Frenchmen, an Irish couple and a Yorkshireman: all hearty-looking types of the sort you find propping up the climbers' bars in Langdale. Their crampons were piled in a corner. 'Sit down, lad,' said the Yorkshireman. 'Get stuck in.'

The Frenchmen were glum. They had just come down from a disastrous climb in the Annapurnas which they had started as three. The third, a lad of 19, had complained of a headache at base camp. They had diagnosed pulmonary oedema, a particularly dangerous form of mountain sickness brought on by fluid in the lungs. The others had immediately evacuated him, but before they could reach a safe altitude he was dead. I knew that pulmonary oedema attacked quickly, but had never heard of anyone suffering from it so severely at only 14,000 feet. It was one of those tragic incidents that would probably never be fully explained. I sympathised as best I could with the two who would now have to go home and face the dead boy's family and friends.

The Irish couple and the Yorkshireman were on their way to an international mountaineering conference in Kathmandu. The Yorkshireman was keen – he was secretary of a well-known British climbing club and obviously felt he had a reputation to keep up. The Irish couple had no such reputation, and were much more casual about the whole affair, which was just as well because they had missed their flight to Kathmandu. 'This is Robin and I'm Síle,' said Síle. She added in a whisper, 'We've really just come along for the ride.'

Next morning, as I explored Delhi with this happy-go-lucky pair, we found we had much in common. Stumbling chaotically around the city, we chanced on world-famous tourist attractions that most people know all about before they even arrive. Not for us the planned itinerary, the informed observation. 'What the dickens is that?' asked Síle as we found ourselves face to face with the Red Fort, venerated for centuries as one of the greatest Moghul monuments of all time. 'No thanks, love,' replied Robin when, on entering the great mosque of Jama Masjid, he was insistently proffered a skirt to cover up his knobbly knees. By this method of trial and error, of *grand panache* and *faux pas*, we saw more of the city in two days than most people find in a fortnight, including many of the merchants' quarters of old Delhi where the streets are named after the things they sell: Silversmiths' Marg, Locksmiths' Marg, and no doubt Transistor Radio Marg and Pocket Calculator Marg too.

Getting around the city was simple and delightful, using the rickshaws whose owners accosted us at every corner – either black and yellow motorised ones that buzzed along on two-stroke engines like giant bumble bees, or pedal ones which were really no more than outsize tricycles. Being European, we had a continuous stream of followers trying to sell us everything from postcards to their grandmothers. At first, I found this difficult to take in my stride. But in most Indians' experience Westerners are rich beyond imagination and gullible beyond belief, so they could hardly be blamed for seeking a little commerce. Robin unwittingly made us see things from their point of view when we came upon two impeccably dressed Arab tourists in front of Rashtrapati Bhavan, the President's magnificent residence, originally the Viceroy's House. 'Look,' he smiled, 'I wonder if they've come to buy the place?'

Of all the things the British left behind in India, I think the

Viceroy's House must have been the most impressive. It was the crowning glory of Edwin Lutyens' architectural career: a symbol of the Empire built of massive sandstone blocks and completed only sixteen years before the British left. There were people who spent their entire working lives building it. Like so many aspects of the British Raj, the Indians have treated it with a curious affection since Independence, and have looked after it so well that now, almost forty years on, it looks better than ever.

Other unlikely reminders of the old days were everywhere. I was taken aback to find traffic driving on the left. Most of it seemed to consist of old Morris Oxfords in various states of repair, and I was glad to hear that thinly disguised versions of these were still being made by the Hindustan Motor Company in Calcutta. Road signs, car number plates and telephones were straight out of *Dr Finlay's Casebook*. Indians adore signs, and devote all their considerable inventive skills to composing them. Almost every streetlamp boasted a slogan exhorting drivers to take more care – to no avail, as far as I could see. 'SLOW DOWN – WE LOVE OUR CHILDREN' was followed by 'LIFE HAS FOUR LETTERS – SO HAS SAFE' and the ubiquitous 'HORN PLEASE' (an utterly superfluous exhortation as anyone who has stood on a Delhi street will know).

As a first step towards Nepal and Kathmandu, I decided to take a train 450 miles down the Ganga – the holy River Ganges – to the city of Varanasi. This wasn't quite as easy as it sounds. India's Northern Railways have some whimsical little rules, one of which is that in Delhi tickets are bought about a mile from the station. The purpose of this is that on arriving in the pell-mell to find your train you are spared having to join the queue of people who haven't got tickets, but are hell-bent on boarding the train anyway – which I noticed most of them managed to do. 'RAILWAY SERVANTS ARE PLEDGED TO SERVE YOU' announced a sign over the platform. As the Yamuna–Ganga Express pulled into Platform Six there were no Railway Servants to be seen, but I did a quick head-count of my fellow passengers and estimated that I would be sharing the train with at least 3,000 people.

The city that now goes by the name of Varanasi was for hundreds of years called Benares, or Banares, or Banaras, and before that, Kashi. It is by general consent the oldest continually occupied settlement on earth. Time and again it appears under one guise or another in India's ancient texts. By the time of the Buddha, about 550 BC, it had become not only a thriving commercial centre but a place of pilgrimage for thousands of Hindus every year. So it was hardly surprising

that the Buddha chose the deer park a few miles away at Sarnath to preach his first great sermon. Mark Twain summed up Varanasi as 'older than history; older than tradition; older even than legend. And looks twice as old as all of them put together'.

The city sits on a great bend of the Ganga, the holy water lapping the steps of the twenty *ghats* or landing stages that make up a waterfront unrivalled, at least in terms of reverence and homage, anywhere in the world. It is a jumble of towers, turrets and domes: some new, some so ancient that they seem to be crumbling back into the Ganga itself. Varanasi stone has a pinkish tinge, and when the sun rises behind the paddy-fields on the opposite bank the river momentarily turns blood red in its reflected glow. The aura is not lost on the pilgrims. Well before the first rays catch the tips of the minarets, the ghats are already thronged with figures come to pray, meditate, defecate and cleanse themselves both spiritually and bodily. By sunrise hundreds of the devout will be found in various stages of undress and immersion as the two great sustainers of life – Surya, the sun, and Ganga, the purifier – symbolically unite. At two of the ghats a different kind of ritual will be in progress: the stoking of the funeral pyres of those who have come to Varanasi to die. As many as a hundred do so every day, because to die here is to escape the vicious circle of reincarnation and pass straight to heaven. Their ashes are shovelled solemnly into the fetid water.

With the followers of two great faiths to cater for, Varanasi is always packed with visitors, and it was with some trepidation that I approached the problem of finding a room. I needn't have worried. The youth who enticed me on to his bicycle rickshaw knew the problem – and the solution. He took off at breakneck speed through a maze of ever narrowing streets, ran over several human toes and one bovine hoof, pressed on bravely and delivered me straight into the arms of Vijay Dixit.

Vijay Dixit, 32 years of age, five feet four, with a shock of jet-black hair and a toe missing, was the proprietor of the Shiva Guest House – 'A PEACEFUL SPOT IN HEART OF THE TOWN. WATER 24 HOURS. ROOMS FILLED WITH SMELL OF GANGES. PLESE DONOT BELIEVE IF RICKSHA DRIVERS AND OTHER YOUNGMAN SAY THAT THE LODGE IS CLOSED.' From modest beginnings he had earned a reputation for unstinting hospitality and helpfulness, not only among Varanasi's religious visitors but with its many foreign 'pilgrims' as well. He prided himself in offering the best tourist information service in Varanasi. No problem was too great, no question too tricky, and if he didn't actually know the answer, which he often didn't, he invented one. I christened him 'Fixit Dixit'.

Fixit Dixit's guest house was indeed filled with the smell of the Ganga, and my room overlooked the great river. I watched sailing barges labour their way upstream in the last of the daylight. One by one the stars came out, and a new moon presented itself artistically left of centre. I wavered. One moment I was completely absorbed; the next I had the

14

distracting feeling that I had blundered into the setting for a play. The Ganga rippled on regardless, barge lights twinkling, the sound of its lapping water drifting by on the evening breeze.

I'm not usually at my best in the morning, so it was with some misgivings that I asked Fixit Dixit to wake me at five. With luck, I thought, he'll probably forget. I was sound asleep when he rattled my door. I blinked at the window shutters showing the first glow of dawn. I hadn't the faintest idea where I was. Then, far away, a rhythmic drumbeat started up; a sitar joined in, and slowly, gently, I was transported back to reality. The Ganga swept darkly past the window. A chatter of voices drifted up as the first pilgrims padded down to the river. I dressed hurriedly and followed them to the main ghat, Dasashwamedh, from where the music was coming.

The sight was extraordinary. In the pre-dawn light two or three hundred people were crowded together on the steps. Their milling bodies went right down to the water's edge, and on into the river until only their heads were visible. For all I could make out they might have carried on further still. Young girls weaved in and out of the crowd, selling mari-golds, rice and the crimson *tika* powder with which Hindus perform the ceremony of *pujaa*. Here at the holiest point on this holiest of rivers this ceremonial daubing would have an added meaning, signifying not only the approval of the great god Shiva but also that of the goddess Ganga herself. A group of pilgrims pushed floating candles out into the river, and swayed gently to the music behind them as they watched their miniature lamps disappear downstream. Another pilgrim, head shaved and wearing only a loincloth, immersed himself in the water and clasped his hands together in prayer, obli-vious to everything except the Ganga and the rising sun. An elderly woman scooped up her sari and waded in to do the same. Alongside her, with less ceremony, a youth soaped his armpits, while thirty yards away old men squatted in a com-munal latrine, ruminating in the sunrise with the same faraway gaze as the worshippers, while passers-by picked their way around them.

By 7 am the city behind the waterfront was already well into its working day. I vied with cycles, rickshaws and spluttering scooters in alleyways designed for no more than pedestrians – and small pedestrians at that. The bells and horns conspired with the shouts of traders to burst my eardrums. I ignored a dozen urgent calls to buy this shirt, inspect that cloth, and concentrated on side-stepping the torrent of wheeled vehicles and staying alive. A cow stood broadside, completely blocking the alley while it thoughtfully nosed through a pile of rotting vegetables in a gutter. The traffic waited impatiently while the sacred animal completed its examination, emptied its bowels in the opposite gutter, and ambled on. '*CHAI?*' shrilled a voice in my ear. I wheeled round to find myself facing a man so old and flimsy I thought at first the question must have come from somebody else. Having got my attention he wasted not a second; with one deft movement he produced a stool, a cushion and a steaming kettle. 'Tea, sir?' he asked.

Quite apart from its religious and historical associations, Varanasi is renowned for its silk, its brassware and (since Ravi Shankar lives there) its sitars. In the lanes I passed shops that were all but enveloped in billowing silks, cheek by jowl with emporia of dazzling copper, silver and brass ornaments, followed by establishments where craftsmen bent lovingly over strange-shaped instruments in various stages of construction. As I passed down the street, the aromas of freshly dyed fabrics gave way to the more pungent smells of resin and sawdust, and as I approached the bazaar both retreated in the face of the familiar rank odour of rotting food. Varanasi entranced me, as it has done others for over 3,000 years, and it was only by the greatest act of will that I continued on my way.

Now anyone with the slightest sense of direction will tell you that it is easy to get from Varanasi to Kathmandu. All you have to do is go to the Nepalese border town of Raxaul, a place served by trains and buses from all points of the compass. But somehow twelve hours after leaving Varanasi I found myself 150 miles too far west. I'm still not quite sure how it happened. I was certain I should go northwards across

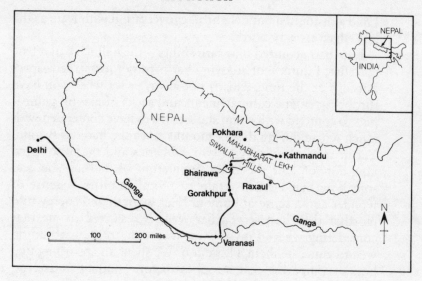

1   Approach to Kathmandu

the Ganga plain to the Indian town of Gorakhpur, then
continue north and east to the border. Arriving at Gorakhpur,
I escaped the mob which crowded round my bus by climbing
on to the only other bus in sight. Everyone agreed that this was
going to Nepal, so I settled down in the front seat and looked
round at my fellow passengers. 'Hello,' said a Lancashire
voice behind me. 'I'm Kate.'

The owner of the voice was in her early twenties: tall,
auburn-haired, with a complexion that might have been
suntan or possibly dust. She grinned and moved forward to sit
beside me. Although I didn't recognise her our paths had
apparently already crossed. She had spotted me in the bus
station in Varanasi, she said, but hadn't realised I was going
the same way as she was. I didn't mention that at that
particular moment neither had I.

A large Nepalese woman settled down on the end of the seat
with a sack of what appeared to be guinea-pigs. She smiled
charmingly and dumped it on my lap. Clutching the wriggling
sack, knees wedged against a throbbing engine compartment,

17

I had a disjointed but delightful conversation with Kate as the bus edged its way north.

Kate had acquired that rare ability – the hallmark of a true traveller, I think – of enjoying her trips not just in retrospect but also at the time. This is not always easy when you have throbbing engine compartments and sacks of playful guinea-pigs to contend with – and she seemed to have contended with much worse during the six months since she had left Britain. Yet in spite of dysentery, two robberies and the unsolicited attention of half the male population of Turkey she had somehow managed to retain two vital faculties, a sense of wonder and a sense of humour. Her warmth and energy told me that they had served her well. It occurred to me that considering where I myself was intending to go, I would do well to cultivate them a little too. We spent an absorbing two hours comparing catastrophes before finding ourselves, almost too quickly, at the Nepalese border post at Bhairawa.

It's curious how when you are in good company problems often seem to melt away. On my own I would have found the hundred or so boys who accosted us, each intent on persuading us to stay at his uncle's B & B, quite disarming. But with Kate's encouragement I swept them amiably aside. The immigration and customs men seemed to share our convivial mood. They chatted for a good half hour about the weather and the price of chapatis before stamping our passports with a flourish and saluting us into Nepal.

Over watery Nepalese beer we discussed our situation. Kate, a model of efficiency, was exactly on course since she was going not to Kathmandu but to Pokhara, the second city of Nepal, 150 miles to the west. I was most impressed, and asked how she did it. She laughed and dug out from the bottom of her pack a battered old school atlas and a magnifying glass. She also reminded me to alter my watch, since Nepal, in a masterly gesture of one-upmanship, keeps its clocks ten minutes ahead of those in India.

My problem resolved itself after a good night's sleep. As Kate's bus pulled out to Pokhara, another one pulled in to the muddy expanse that passed for a bus station. Nepalese buses don't actually say where they are going, but it was obvious from the chatter that this one was going to Kathmandu. With Russian, American, Canadian and British help, Nepal was building an east–west road across its part of the Ganga plain, and the bus would make use of the recently completed British section to reach the road from Raxaul. We lurched out of the bus station, the passengers babbling happily in a mixture of Hindi, Nepali and (for my benefit) some horribly contorted English. We would, they assured me, be in Kathmandu by nightfall.

After a while the labouring engine and grinding gears began to suggest that we were beginning to climb. Aroused from my snooze, I looked hopefully in the direction where the mountains should have been, but it was a few seconds before I thought to tilt my head. Then I saw them. Forest green and ice white, they soared into a different dimension. I fell back in my seat and the other passengers laughed.

When the explorer Don Cortés was asked to describe his newly discovered Mexico to the King of Spain, he crumpled a piece of paper in his fist. 'That is the map of Mexico,' he said. He could equally have been talking about Asia. Not just the Himalaya, but range after range of peaks radiate from northeast Kashmir westwards across Afghanistan and eastwards across India and Tibet. The western ranges are arid and gaunt; these are the Karakoram and the mountains of Ladakh, Zanskar and the Hindu Kush. The eastern ones are snowy, with humid forested valleys. Further east still the Tibetan ranges curve south into one of the most inaccessible areas of the world. These are the mountains of the Chinese–Burmese border that give rise to the great rivers Irrawaddy and Mekong, draining Thailand and Laos and eventually disgorging into the China Sea. I was now looking up at the most rugged part of this piece of crumpled paper – the central Himalaya.

The bus wound its way through the Siwalik foothills and soon we were crossing the high plain that forms the pediment of the first big range, Mahabharat Lekh. The Nepalese were making good use of this flat land and growing rice or maize on every square foot. People were everywhere, steering ox-drawn ploughs, scything corn, or threshing the grain with great sticks in the shade of banana plants and avocado trees. I thought of the last time I had been riding across a high plateau under snow-capped peaks, in Peru. There the Quechua and Aymará Indians had gone about lethargically under a vertical sun, working just to keep themselves alive. Here, away from the tropics, people had a vigour and vitality which made you want to join in.

We dived into a gorge and the sun went out. Grey glacial water swept between vertical cliffs. I climbed on to the roof of the bus to get a better view, and noticed that above me the sky had turned grey too. Storm clouds boiled above my head, hiding the rim of the gorge so that we seemed to be driving through a huge grey tunnel. Of course. Early October. The last of the monsoon rains. Then the water hit me.

The monsoon in southern Asia is one of the few things in that part of the world which usually comes on time. On the southern slopes of the Himalaya it can be relied upon, most years, to arrive during the last week of June and to deposit regular amounts of heavy rain in the valleys and on the lower peaks until the end of September. I had hoped to arrive after these rains had petered out, so had tucked my raingear deep down at the bottom of my pack. In any case my pack was buried under mounds of trunks, sacks, spare wheels and a cast-iron mangle on the roof-rack behind me. I was soaked within seconds. The bus didn't stop. Even if it had done I would have got just as wet inside, because it didn't have a windscreen. The road hugged the river-bank; the bus hugged the road; I hugged the bus. A suspension bridge came briefly into view, carrying the Pokhara road. We turned east, away from Pokhara, and started to climb. It got cold and I huddled against the mangle, nibbling the sugar-cane that was sticking out of it. It was in this sorry but very appropriate state that I arrived in Kathmandu.

Kathmandu lies 4,500 feet above sea level in a broad valley which, it is said, was once a lake. The lake was called Nag Hrad, which means Lake of Serpents, and legend tells us that it was indeed full of serpents and snakes, not to mention gods such as Bipaswi Buddha, who was often to be seen going in and out among the lotus plants which covered its waters. A little before the beginning of recorded history the valley was visited by a great king from the north, Manjusri, who was looking for a place for his people to live. Nag Hrad fitted the bill, and Manjusri decided to drain the lake so his people could cultivate its fertile alluvial bed. He drew his sword and cut a gorge through Mahabharat Lekh to the south, and the waters swept away towards the Ganga, taking the serpents and snakes with them. The place where his sword landed is to this day called Chobar ('Sword-cut'). Manjusri's people prospered in the hospitable climate and reaped good harvests from the rich soil. They founded Manjupatan ('Manjusri's Town'), now simply called Patan.

The first clearly recorded event happened in 1614, when King Lakshmi Narsingh built a wooden guest house on the bank of Bagmati Khola (the River Bagmati) for his visitors. It became known as Kasthmandap, the Square House of Wood, and the city around it came to be called Kathmandu. The valley's three settlements of Kathmandu, Patan and Bhaktapur were at this time actually ruled as independent kingdoms, even though a person could walk from one to either of the others in less than two hours. The kingdoms had their own legal systems, art, architecture, festivals – even their own coinage. They survived in this way until the Gurkhas from the west overran the valley in the eighteenth century and created what is now Nepal. But even today each city has its own customs and distinct atmosphere, though Patan has been engulfed by the ever-expanding suburbs of Kathmandu.

To anyone brought up in the 1960s, the name Kathmandu has a magical ring – like Woodstock, San Francisco or Monterey. Almost untouched by Western culture, it must have been a memorable place to reach after a long overland trip. But I think Kathmandu's heyday was probably a little earlier, in the 1950s. Its only links with the outside world then were mule trails, its only motor cars a couple belonging to King Tribhuvan. These had been carried over the mountains bit by bit by porters and pack animals. They were brought out only on state occasions, and then they had to be pushed, because there was no petrol.

Slowly things changed. The road from India came in the 1960s, and from China in the 1970s. The influx of immigrants along these roads (refugees in the case of the latter one, after China occupied Tibet in 1959) gave the Nepalese of the Kathmandu Valley a more cosmopolitan outlook. Their natural gregariousness and hospitality made them quick to accept the newcomers and their strange ways. The Tibetans soon became regarded as brothers and sisters, the few Western tourists as odd but distinguished cousins. The needs of both were accommodated without fuss.

I clambered down from the roof of the bus, retrieved my sodden pack and sloshed off to find somewhere to stay. I could have had my pick of at least fifty hotels, lodges or uncles' guest houses if I had listened to any of the boys who besieged me in the first hundred yards, but I declined them all. The streets were empty except for several inches of water. Faces grinned at me from shops and tea-houses. I crossed Durbar Square in front of the old royal palace and walked through a forest of temples, raindrops dripping by the thousand from their pagoda roofs. I wandered up Indrachowk into the heart of the old city in search of a hotel where I could rest unmolested for a few days. Even here there were few passers-by. Everybody had fled for shelter and I had the narrow winding streets to myself. I reached the Thamel district where many of the cheaper hotels are, and finally put down my pack in the aptly named Pheasant Lodge, where pheasants scratched around among the puddles in the yard and a pink rabbit with floppy ears peered inquisitively at me from a cage.

It rained hard all night. I could hear it playing music on the tin roof of the rabbit's cage. However, when I awoke next morning I was delighted to find that the rain had stopped, the sun was high in the sky and the remains of the puddles were steaming. I dressed quickly and excitedly, then stepped out of the Pheasant Lodge and stopped in my tracks.

Where previously the street had been deserted except for some abandoned bicycles and a couple of ducks, there was now a surging mass of tourists of every nationality and creed. Levis, sunglasses, sports jackets, cameras, handbags, guide-books – even a stetson, a kaftan and a tee-shirt saying 'I've FLOWN OVER EVEREST'. No kidding. Wall to wall. As I gaped, flabbergasted, I noticed Nepalese boys weaving through the crowd hawking prayer-wheels, beads and other trinkets. The tourists were buying them by the dozen.

'You like?' A diminutive figure offered me a cheaply carved *khukri*, the traditional curved Nepalese knife. 'I ask only 200 rupees,' the boy said.

'Hey man,' came over my shoulder from another youth. 'You want hash? You want pretty girl? You got dollars?'

I had seen 'megatourism' in Third World countries before, but never anything quite like this. In Peru, for instance, the stoical Quechua and Aymará Indians keep the worst jet-set image-seekers at bay by the simple tactic of being aloof. The Nepalese, on the other hand, are naturally friendly and hospi-table people, and born traders. They are well aware that most tourists come for the 'legend' of Kathmandu, and they nurture this legend wonderfully. The ethnic flavour is just enough to titillate the taste buds, without being so sharp that it frightens the more timid tourists away. Like all natural talents, it comes to them without their even being aware of it. Nepal now receives an incredible quarter of a million tourists each year. Many of them – by Nepalese standards – spend their dollars, pounds or Deutschmarks like confetti, and King Birendra's government would understandably like to attract still more. I took a last look at this awful, pathetic scene, dodged another boy peddling marijuana, and escaped down a side street.

My plan was to do a short 'dummy run' to test my equipment, get myself fit, and hopefully get some idea of the kinds of problems I would be likely to encounter on the walk itself. Then I would come back to Kathmandu and spend two or three weeks learning sufficient Nepali to ask directions and buy food along the way. This would also be an opportunity to arrange my visa extension, buy supplies and make any final adjustments to my gear. It was now the second week of October, so I reckoned I should be ready to start the walk in mid to late November, by which time the monsoon would be well and truly over. The only trouble with this plan was that from December onwards, there was a real chance that the high passes along the route would be blocked by snow. Some of them, once closed, would not reopen until the spring. It definitely looked as if it was going to be a race against time.

For my dummy run I chose the Annapurna Circuit. This was a 150 mile walk encircling the Annapurna massif via the Marsyangdi and Thak Khola valleys, which were linked by the 17,500 foot Thorung La pass. The circuit would be long enough to give me a foretaste of the actual walk, and the pass would acclimatise me for those I would be crossing later on. Also, the circuit went through some places that were very interesting in their own right. Sixty miles up the Marsyangdi Khola, it crossed an arid region behind the Annapurnas called Nyesyang where Manangba traders still enjoyed exemption from customs duties by virtue of an eighteenth-century royal proclamation. Beyond the Thorung La, it entered the once independent Mustang district where Buddhists of the Sakya-pa sect until thirty years ago paid homage and taxes to the King of Lo. It passed Muktinath, an ancient shrine where hot springs and natural gases have been venerated by Hindu and Buddhist pilgrims from all over southern Asia for at least 2,500 years. And it offered the possibility of making a detour into the so-called Annapurna Sanctuary, where I could gain some experience of living at 14,000 feet surrounded by several of the highest mountains in the world. Most important of all, at least half the Annapurna Circuit had only recently been opened to trekkers, so I hoped it wouldn't be too badly afflicted by the tourist atrocities I had just seen in Kathmandu. How wrong I was to be proved to be!

Patriotic Englishmen abroad, so I had read, should at some stage during their visit present themselves at the British Embassy and pay their respects to Her Majesty's Ambassador or Consul. This seemed to me rather an impractical suggestion, and very hard on the ambassadors and consuls, but never let it be said that I am not a good patriot. That afternoon found me pressing the small brass bell-push at the Embassy gates on Lazimpath, and being told that the Vice-Consul, Mr Fulton, would see me in a few minutes. How clever, I thought, to appoint a vice-consul to handle all these patriotic people; the obvious solution.

Jim Fulton turned out to be one of the few people in Nepal who fully understood my trip. He ushered me into his office and offered me an easy chair. Blue Scottish eyes examined me from behind wire-rimmed spectacles. 'So you've come to write about north-west Nepal? I don't think any of our chaps have ever been there. It will certainly give you lots of material for your book.' He gave a little grin. 'I hope you have a successful and trouble-free trip. I say that from the bottom of my heart, because if you don't, I'm the one who will have to repatriate your body.'

3

Dummy Run

> 'Look after the molehills, and the mountains
> will look after themselves.'
> Laurence J. Peter and Raymond Hull,
> *The Peter Principle*

Most people, if you ask them what sticks out most in their memories of Kathmandu, will recall the fabulous architecture of the temples and old houses, or the stunning backdrop of the Himalaya, or the mingling in the streets of ethnic groups from all over southern Asia. I have to admit that my main memory is of pizza. Since the so-called hippie invasion of the late 1960s, Kathmandu's entrepreneurs have discovered that the way to the hearts of their visitors is through their stomachs. Restaurants have multiplied to the extent that in at least two streets of the city there is now little else. These two streets, officially called Jhochhen and Maru Tole, are affectionately known by everyone as Freak Street and Pig Alley. Here the hungry traveller can find restaurants rejoicing in names like 'Paradise', 'Cosmopolitan' and 'Eat at Joe's', with menus offering spaghetti bolognese, hamburgers and a wondrous assortment of pies, cakes and flans – all dished up to what their Nepalese proprietors like to think is the very latest in Western rock music, usually 10-year-old Abba.

I quickly established my loyalties with a place called 'K.C.'s'. As far as pizza was concerned, K.C. seemed to have a chef's instinct not often found outside Italy, and considerably aided by the fact that he had cornered the Nepalese market in mozzarella cheese. He had also managed to lay his hands on the few tapes in Kathmandu that weren't Abba. Some time after my meeting with Jim Fulton I sat in 'K.C.'s' toying with my pizza margherita and side salad, and making a shopping list: I was due to leave next morning for the Annapurna Circuit.

I really had no idea what to expect. Everybody gave conflicting advice. The trekking outfitters in Thamel said it was impossible to do the full circuit without ropes and crampons; the tour agencies in Durbar Marg said I would need a guide and porters. The boss at my hotel, who also ran a small grocery shop, considered rather predictably that I should take food for several weeks. In New York, I believe they tell you that the only way to do this trek is to fly to Jomosom by special charter. On the principle that the only reliable informants would be people who had done the walk themselves, I cautiously inquired of the dozen or so other customers in the restaurant.

By now I had learned to recognise people who had been trekking. They were generally thin, unkempt, with a hint of madness in their eyes and a layer of grime on their clothes and skin. And they were always hungry. In between mouthfuls of margherita and forkfuls of fruit flan no less than six people said yes, they had been on one part or another of the Annapurna Circuit. Two were Japanese and intensely engaged in some kind of business deal with K.C. – perhaps importing Sony Walkmen to sell to trekkers. The other four were rugged-looking Canadians who had just spent six weeks north of Annapurna – in exactly the area that worried me most. They reckoned I would need to be self-sufficient for three days to cross the Thorung La pass, if I was lucky and didn't get snowed in. Elsewhere I would have few problems because there would be tea-houses along the way. The key to it all was to do the circuit anticlockwise, to avoid an impossible ascent from Muktinath to the top of the pass. This meant I should start at Dumre, a village on the Pokhara road about five hours from Kathmandu. I could buy some last-minute things in Dumre, but would be best to stock up with my basic supplies in Kathmandu.

As a life support system for a snowstorm on the Thorung La

> ## Shopping list
>
> Flour for chapatis
> Lentils - red + green
> Sikkim tea (the best!)
> Powdered milk - get from
>   Lamchaur dairy
> Sugar - lots.
> Rice
> Supplementary medical kit -
>   tincture of opium - see the
>   shaman re: herbal medicines.
>
> Packet soups from shops in Thamel
> Nuts + dried fruit
> Ingredients for DIY muesli
> Potatoes
> Sweets ← the kids call
>   them mithai.
> Salt + pepper
> 'Three Ekka' matches
> Spare bootlaces
> Candles!

pass, the list seemed pitifully short. But I was laden down with the tent, sleeping bag, cooking stove and other paraphernalia I had brought from Britain, and at forty-five pounds my pack was already a lot heavier than I was used to. Five pounds of food was definitely the limit.

In fact the Nepalese rarely measure things in pounds. More often they use *maanaa*, a unit which is related to how much of a given commodity one can reap from a certain area of land. As the area used varies from one part of Nepal to another, and the amount one can reap depends on the climate, the soil and what crop one is talking about, the maanaa is a very flexible amount and always open to negotiation between buyer and seller. In Kathmandu an attempt has been made, not very successfully, to standardise it by introducing brass measuring bowls for the more common things like rice and lentils. I even saw some weighing scales marked in kilos. But old ways die hard, and I bought most of my supplies from the bazaar in quantities that dated back 2,000 years, from men and women who looked as if they might well have been around when they were introduced. For these items I would be asked so many *sukaa* (25 paisaa or a quarter of a rupee) or *mohar* (50 paisaa). The shopkeepers made it clear that they expected me to haggle, and prompted me as to how hard a bargain I might drive – all of which was rather pointless since I had not yet learned how to read the numerals on the coins.

Eventually I had everything on my list, and on an impulse bought two final things – from a Tibetan store, a roll of toilet paper aptly labelled 'Yeti Brand'; and from the dusty recesses of an expedition outfitter's in Thamel, wonder of wonders, a Mars bar. The latter was as hard as stone and looked as if it

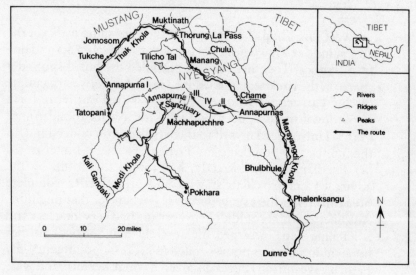

2 The dummy run

might have been a relic from Edmund Hillary's days. However, I thought, if it proved inedible I could always use it as a rock belay.

The bus to Dumre, like most Nepalese buses, left at 6 am. Of course, it didn't really. That was the time by which all the passengers were supposed to be in their seats, whereupon it tore round the city, revving and tooting wildly to make sure everyone was awake, then waited for another hour just in case any last-minute passengers should come by.

I left for the bus station by rickshaw – not because I had any pretentions to style, but because I couldn't lift my pack. The bus was waiting in the pre-dawn mist. I paid the rickshaw driver and stepped on board, to be greeted by a sea of white faces.

'Hi! Hello! Where 'ya heading?'

'Er, Dumre.'

'Great, so are we.'

'The Annapurna Circuit?'

'Yep.'

'Oh.'

Sweet joy. I had chosen to start the very same walk on the very same day as two huge parties, one from Nebraska and one from France. Together they all but filled the bus. I spotted a space on the back seat and wedged myself in between a couple of chic Parisiennes who seemed to be kitted out more for a stroll down the Rue de Rivoli than for a walk round Annapurna. I introduced myself to them (solely, you understand, in the interests of practising my French). Gertie, if I interpreted her Parisian accent correctly, had joined the group on the advice of her psychiatrist who had prescribed a complete break from her life as a *promotrice* – whatever that might be. Antoinette, who I couldn't help noticing had very long legs and a fetching lisp, informed me severely that she was on her honeymoon. At this point – much to my disappointment – my French gave out, so I never discovered where her husband was.

The only couple who weren't from Nebraska or France turned out to be from that legendary cradle of mountaineering prowess, Manchester. Above the cacophony, their clipped Lancashire tones came through louder and clearer by the minute. Wendy and George were having what I think in marital circles is called a tiff. It obviously hadn't occurred to them that anyone on the bus might possibly understand what they were saying. I strained my ears.

The argument seemed to revolve around the walk they were about to do. Wendy was all for taking it slowly, a few miles a day, and enjoying the scenery even if they didn't make it over the pass. George, on the other hand, obviously regarded it as a challenge and was planning their assault like a military campaign.

'If we can average twenty kilometres a day we should just about do it,' he said, nose deep in map.

'But if we have to average twenty kilometres a day I don't *want* to do it,' wailed Wendy. And so they continued, he the aggressive one, she the reluctant one. I took a secret bet on who would win.

Having found no more passengers by 7.30 am, we finally left the city and I settled back to enjoy the ride. Squeezed in between Gertie and Antoinette, this wasn't difficult. But I did manage to divert my attention from Antoinette's legs sufficiently to notice that the road to Dumre was in a sorry state of repair. Repair was hardly the word for what they were doing to it, which seemed to involve large gangs of men laboriously filling potholes with dried buffalo dung. This was having singularly little effect, and as the hours passed by the bumps grew steadily more violent. It became too bumpy to read; it even became too bumpy to look at Antoinette's legs.

Mercifully we stopped in every village along the way, and at each stop we were sitting targets for small boys selling bananas. As the journey progressed I became quite a connoisseur of these (the bananas, that is). They ranged from pathetic brown stubs which had obviously failed to meet even the fairly relaxed standards of the village shopkeepers, to immense phalluses that were almost bursting out of their skins. With Gertie on one side and Antoinette on the other, I found it difficult to take a bite out of the latter without blushing.

The road from Kathmandu to Dumre and Pokhara is one of life's great adventures. Little more than ten feet wide, it winds over a pass and along the edges of precipices whose impact on the impressionable traveller is heightened by the many wayside crosses commemorating those who have gone over the edge. While rounding a particularly nasty blind bend our driver took both hands off the wheel and pointed excitedly into the canyon below. We craned our necks and could just make out the wreckage of a bus in similar colours to our own. The driver turned gleefully towards us, hands still off the wheel. 'That was last Tuesday's bus,' he said.

Dumre is one of several villages that have sprung up since the Kathmandu to Pokhara road was completed by the Chinese in 1973. It is not much of a place, but acts as a staging post for goods and travellers from an area of no less than 2,000 square miles. I asked for the Marsyangdi Valley path, and was shown a muddy lane which left the main street between two houses. The French had gone off to find their porters, the Nebraskans were complaining that it wasn't a touch on Omaha, and Wendy and George were still arguing about kilometres. I shouldered my pack, hoping to make my escape while none of them was looking. I took a few steps up the lane and keeled over.

It took me a moment to realise what had happened. I lay on my back, pinned down helplessly by my pack, arms and legs flailing like an upturned beetle. A crowd of Nepalese boys gathered round me, grinning. This sort of thing obviously happened regularly in Dumre. Some of the Nebraskans came over to see what was going on. It obviously didn't happen much in Omaha. I don't know if it happened in Manchester, because Wendy and George carried on arguing, oblivious to the world.

As I lay wondering what to do next, a very old lady elbowed her way through the crowd. She had a hunched back, lots of wrinkles and a gold ring through her nose. She shooed everyone away, Nepalese and Nebraskans alike, proffered me a strong, bony arm and helped me to my feet. She pointed to a thatched wooden house across the street. I lugged my leaden pack as far as her front porch and sank on to a bench. My first attempt at the Annapurna Circuit had lasted just twenty yards.

I had been hopelessly optimistic in estimating what I could carry. My pack weighed well over fifty pounds; heaven knows how much that was in maanaa. The old lady and I went through its contents one by one. She suggested I throw out most of the food and several items of clothing which were nearing the end of their useful life. By the time I had finished the villagers of Dumre were a good deal better off and the pack weighed ten pounds less. Moreover, I found to my delight that I could just carry it without toppling over. My fellow bus passengers had all disappeared up the lane. Without further ado, I hastened after them.

Dumre, eighty miles from the source of the Marsyangdi, lies only 1,500 feet above sea level; one of the lowest spots in the whole of the Himalaya. The October afternoon was hot and devastatingly humid. I trudged along, sometimes on a wide track rutted by jeeps, sometimes through paddy-fields green with tall summer rice. At several of the houses along the way tables had been set out, offering oranges, coconuts, papaya and sugar-cane to quench the traveller's thirst.

The path itself was a hubbub of activity, with a constant stream of people on the move. Heading uphill, porters from the villages of the Magar and Newar people to the south were bent under loads of sugar, rice and other lowland products which would be sold to the villagers of the upper valleys. Coming down, the porters were of Tibetan origin and carried cargoes of wool, woven goods and occasionally some rancid yak butter in old mustard seed oil cans. Where I had been complaining about my fifty pound rucksack with its comfortably padded hip belt and shoulder straps, these porters had only a crude conical wicker basket to support their loads. This *doko* was carried by means of a *naamlo* – a broad tump-line across the forehead, which requires outrageously strong neck muscles to keep the doko at the correct angle. I say this with some confidence because I tried.

Porters command great respect among the hill people of Nepal, because apart from their impressive stamina they are the villagers' lifeline to the outside world. They are staunch and proud and inseparable from their dokos, which they fuss over like mother hens, adjusting a line here and a rope there. I saw both boys and girls carrying dokos from the age of about two. For all I know they may be born with them on. The porters I met walked barefoot, having long since worn out any shoes they might once have possessed. I followed their big flat footprints along the muddy path, hypnotised. They themselves would plod doggedly along in groups of four or six, steadying themselves with a stout walnut pole hewn by their khukris into the shape of an elongated T. Every few hundred yards they would stop for a minute's rest, using their poles like shooting sticks to support the dokos which, when fully loaded, might weigh up to 120 pounds.

I decided to make my first night's stop at a village with the tantalising name of Phalenksangu. This is a corruption of the English word *plank* (as heard through Nepalese ears) coupled with the Nepali word *sangu* which means a rather primitive sort of bridge. As most bridges in Nepal are rather primitive, I was looking forward to seeing what the Nepalese considered a primitive one. I asked regularly how far it was, and each time got the same reply.

'It is just around the corner, sahib.'

I rounded twenty corners in this way, confidently expecting to see the plank bridge, only to be told again that it was just around the corner. I stopped briefly for some papaya and hurried on. The sun was low in the late afternoon sky but it was still roasting my unfit and unprepared body. Sweat poured down my forehead and dripped from my chin on to my chest.

'It is just around the corner, sahib.'

The sun set in a blaze of splendour that was by now lost on me. I stumbled on through the darkness, and an hour later arrived in Phalenksangu, all in. Stubborn idiocy had got me there. Excruciating pains were coming from my back, head and feet, in that order. I crumpled on the doorstep of the first house I came to. Looking up, I noticed that it described itself, rather grandly I thought, as the Krishna Hotel. But I was past caring, and lay still.

Suddenly the lady of the house was standing over me, babbling in Nepali. 'Well, dear me,' she twittered (or something like that). 'Here's another half-dead walker. Come in you poor thing and have a glass of tea.'

The sweet spiced tea went straight into my bloodstream. I perked up a little and asked for some more. As I drank a second and then a third glass, my hostess bustled over her stove and tut-tutted like my mother used to when I had been out playing in the rain. Her family of five gathered in a circle and prodded at my rucksack. 'Would you like some supper?' she asked in a tone that indicated she would be very cross if I said no. She was obviously not a woman to be argued with. I sank back gratefully against her mud wall, and practised my Nepali on the children while supper cooked.

Nepali is one of the five major Devanagari languages of southern Asia. Although Indo-Aryan in origin – that is, from south of the Himalaya – it has for centuries been understood (more or less) by the Tibetan people to the north. Within Nepal itself there are untold variations, and a Kiranti from the east has about as much chance of understanding a Tarap from the west as a Japanese student of English might have of deciphering Geordie. Much of its vocabulary is derived directly from Sanskrit, the ancient language of the Indian subcontinent. Other words have been borrowed from Persian, Hindi and, more recently, English. Educated Nepalese are said to favour Sanskrit words – a result no doubt of the translation of the popular Hindu epics, the *Ramayana* and the *Mahabharata*.

Only in the last forty years have efforts been made to transcribe Nepali into Roman characters. The spellings are splendidly variable. Many of them are courageous attempts to express sounds unknown to the European or American ear, like *chh*, a cross between 'ch' and 'ts', and *Th*, an unearthly clicking sound which only the Nepalese seem to be able to do properly. Among other things, these discrepancies mean that Westerners are doomed to speak Nepali badly.

Taking advantage of the children's undivided attention, I experimented with the few words I had learned so far: hello, goodbye, the numbers one to ten, please, thank you, yes and no. I was doing reasonably well until it came to yes and no. In the dialect of the Marsyangdi Valley yes is indicated by *ah*, no by *aha*. My natural tendency to come out with one or the other of these whenever I'm making up my mind what to say next had the children rolling about in merry disbelief.

Like most Nepalese houses, this was of two storeys – the lower one a single, simply furnished room which acted as kitchen, dining room and living accommodation, the upper one really no more than a loft with a few rough-hewn bunks for sleeping. Although the house's walls were of mud its frame was of heavier timber, giving it a solid look which was further accentuated by a spectacular corrugated iron roof. This hideous material, imported extensively from India, has done much to disfigure the appearance of Nepalese villages over the last twenty years. Its offensiveness to Western eyes is a profound mystery to those Nepalese lucky enough to be able to afford it, who charmingly quell criticisms from their foreign visitors by pointing out its effectiveness in keeping out the rain.

My hostess, Jashara Maya, had all the characteristics of a well-to-do woman of the hills. The fierce pride of her Magar ancestors had been mellowed by living in this relatively fertile valley, and, more recently, by the prosperity brought by trekkers like me. She wore her dowry proudly – a necklace of amber and jade, earrings of silver and a great gold disc in her nose. Her black hair was plaited with woollen braids dyed scarlet, which bobbed and bounced in flashes of colour as she busied herself around the stove. Her clothes were in similar contrast: black blouse and skirt, with an emerald green shawl and scarlet cummerbund. Her face creased into a hundred wrinkles as she grinned expansively and announced that supper was ready.

As the guest I was served first, and was expected to show my approval before anyone else would eat. This wasn't difficult; the aromas coming from Jashara Maya's stove had already told me she was an excellent cook. On the table she set out a large bowl of rice, a smaller one of lentils, an even smaller one of spiced cabbage and, on a saucer, a tiny piece of chicken. '*Daal bhaat tarkaari!*' she announced triumphantly. Daal bhaat I knew was rice and lentils, the Nepalese staple diet. You pour the lentils over the rice and eat it with your fingers. The people of the hills have this basic but surprisingly nourishing meal almost every day of their lives. The other dishes – the tarkaari or spiced cabbage and the chicken – were extra for the English guest. I reflected that the chicken had probably been flapping up and down the village street only that morning.

We had been joined by a few others for supper, and I was fascinated to find that one was the valley postman. I have always found it difficult to believe that post can come and go in such remote places – or indeed anywhere not served by a little red van – but this worthy gentleman ran the mail along seventy miles of trail between Pokhara and Manang. Collections and deliveries were made once a month, weather and harvesting commitments permitting. At peak periods like Tibetan New Year he had the services of a yak.

One of the others at supper was a dark-looking character. He watched me intently while I ate, then paid for his meal and left without a word. Jashara Maya was agitated. 'That man is a robber,' she snorted, grabbing my arm and shaking it to make sure I understood. 'He has stolen from many foreign visitors and is often violent. You must be very careful tonight.' I knew from past experience that stories of violence and robbery are often terribly exaggerated, especially in remote places where they may be the biggest news for months. But I was a bit unnerved by her concern, and it was still on my mind when, an hour later, I said goodnight and climbed the ladder to my bunk in the loft.

In the flickering light of an oil lamp, a dark figure lay asleep on my bed. The robber! I scrambled back down and dragged the others to see. They clambered cautiously over the rim of the loft, holding their breath. Peering through the gloom, Jashara Maya approached the sleeping figure, then suddenly burst out laughing. 'That's Grandfather. You've taken his bed!'

By morning, thankfully, all was forgotten. Jashara Maya was up at 4.30, and through the cracks in the floorboards I could see her going about her morning housework. This consisted, after kindling the fire, of washing down the walls and floor and giving them a liberal coating of mud mixed with buffalo dung. The work was done by the light of a single candle while the rest of the family snored. After a moment of indignation at the injustice of this, I'm ashamed to say I joined them.

Breakfast − served at the civilised hour of 8 am − would have been described by a more progressive hotelier as 'Hearty English'. As well as boiled eggs and unlimited quantities of her sweet spiced tea, Jashara Maya served up *roti* (a Nepalese form of chapati) and a delicious substance which, with eyes closed and a little imagination, could have passed for Robertson's Golden Shred. It was difficult to pull myself away from her splendid hospitality, and my legs worked reluctantly to carry me on up the valley.

The Marsyangdi Khola is typical of those draining the

southern slopes of the Himalaya. In its lower reaches every square foot of its valley is planted with rice. The paddy-fields rise without a break from the banks of the river to the highest tops of the surrounding hills. Around the villages are clumps of banana plants and orange trees and, looking rather incongruous, an occasional plot of potatoes.

Until recently these valleys were self-sufficient and played no part in the economy of Nepal. Now, as they are being swept into greater contact and less independence, their traditional strengths and weaknesses are being turned on their heads. In the village squares, instead of talking about last year's harvest or the prospects for this year's, the men discuss unemployment and the strength of the rupee.

But if all this sounds depressingly familiar, let me mention a better piece of news that I heard wherever I went. The government's attempts to end the feudal system were, people said, at last beginning to work. The system was a legacy of the Rana prime ministers who ruled for more than a century until 1951, and who seem to have behaved rather like European monarchs in the Middle Ages, handing out gifts of land to friends and supporters in return for political favours. In this way, over the years, most of Nepal had fallen into the hands of just a few families, and ground rents of up to 80 per cent of the land's produce were extracted from the unfortunate farmers. Now 'Land Reform' was on everybody's lips. Limits had been established to how much land an individual could own and how much produce he or she could charge as rent. Sub-tenancies had been abolished, accumulated debts liquidated, and the land was being redistributed slowly (too slowly, some said) to the people who actually farmed it. For the first time in living memory farmers had an incentive to use the soil to the full. One immediate effect was that after the rice crops had been harvested in November and December, many now planted their paddy-fields with winter wheat.

On the path ahead I spotted two familiar figures. They were moving slowly, and they were still arguing. I trotted up alongside and got the gist of the discussion which had now taken on a new turn. Wendy was in tears. 'I don't like eating rice all the time, I don't like sleeping on hard floors, and I've got a funny feeling that I don't like being here with you.'

George didn't seem to have heard. 'If we get another five kilometres under our belts before lunch, we might just make Bhulbhule tonight,' he announced.

We continued for a few minutes in awkward silence. Suddenly Wendy sat down on a rock. 'My rucksack's broken,' she said triumphantly.

The fracture was in an unfortunate place, just at the point on the frame where one of the shoulder straps was attached. George looked exasperated. Wendy looked at her feet.

Finally George said, 'Look, I'll carry it to Bhulbhule under my arm. With luck, we'll be able to get it fixed there, and still make it up to the pass in five days.' With this he marched off: one pack on his back, one under his arm, steam coming out of his ears.

'He's probably hungry,' sighed Wendy. 'He always gets cross when he's hungry.'

The village of Bhulbhule, named after a small Himalayan bird with a loud voice, is pronounced 'Woolly-Bully' – like the song. We arrived just after dark, George still lugging the two packs. He looked dreadful, and I was in a pretty bad state too. The aches and pains that had been dogging me since Dumre had now broken out in a violent fever. We found a tea-house and I collapsed in a corner, sweat pouring down my face. Wendy gave me codeine and forced me to drink some water, while the village ladies peered inquisitively over her shoulder and suggested other remedies in a motherly way. One idea rather appealed to me, since it involved persuading the village *shaman* or medicine man to stand outside the tea-house and beat his drum. Even if this didn't completely cure me by driving away the spirits that were causing my fever, it would at least have driven away these zealous ladies which, I felt, would have been a good start.

For two days I lay and sweated, rising only to vomit through the open window of the tea-house which fortunately gave out straight over the river. I thought at first I must have caught malaria. (I've had a romantic ambition to perish heroically from something like that ever since I read Alan Moorehead's *The White Nile*.) However, Wendy dashed all my hopes of an illustrious demise by telling me that I was suffering from nothing worse than dehydration. I had done too much, too quickly in the debilitating heat. My body needed time to adjust. All I had to do was lie still and drink lots of tea.

On the third morning I made an excursion to test my legs. The fever had weakened me and they were pathetically wobbly; I floundered around Bhulbhule like an old drunk. But I felt I had outstayed my welcome at the tea-house, and it was time to move on. I could walk all right unladen, but when I put on my pack I crumpled to the ground. It looked very much as if I was going to have to hire a porter.

Although I had passed hundreds of porters along the way, the idea of actually asking one to carry my luggage took some getting used to. On the trails I had been on in South America porters had been few and far between, and in Africa, the only other continent where I had come across them, the arrangements had always had a distinctly colonial ring. How could I hire a porter when I didn't even have a pith helmet?

Ram Bahadur, the youth who offered me his services, made it clear that he didn't mind if I had a pith helmet or even a couple of goats in my pack, so long as I paid him a fair wage. We settled on thirty rupees a day (about £1.40 sterling) plus food. He set off like greased lightning, skipping along barefoot, grinning from ear to ear. I took up the rear in shorts and boots, issuing instructions loudly in the spirit of Livingstone. In this way we proceeded for the next three days, successfully if not exactly smoothly, to the town of Chame.

Ram Bahadur's appetite was gargantuan – a real expense account job. Twice a day we would stop for daal bhaat, and he would put away mounds of rice washed down with as many glasses of sweet spiced tea as I would allow him. I also treated him to an occasional tot of *rakshi*, an illicit but very popular

Nepalese spirit looking and tasting exactly like Esso Blue, which increased his horsepower dramatically.

Chame is the administrative centre for the district of Manang. It came as quite a shock when, a week from the nearest road, I walked up its stone-paved main street and saw hotels, government offices and even a branch of the Bank of Nepal. It was strange too to see the word *Manang* used here because I knew that the village of Manang, home of the ethnically and culturally distinct Manangba people, was at least two days' walk further on. Here in Chame the people were a mixture of Manangba from the north and Magar, Newar and Tamang from the south.

Feeling still a bit weak from my fever, I made my excuses to the host at my lodging and retired early to bed. I awoke an hour later to find myself alone in the house. Half-empty glasses of rakshi stood on the table; the fire was still burning in the hearth. It looked very much as if the proprietor, his friends and Ram Bahadur had gone off on a Nepalese pub crawl.

Next morning all were back safely, sleeping like babies. Ram Bahadur was the first to rise, which he did with some difficulty, clutching his head. Soon my host was up too, bustling about and trying to hide his hangover. He explained that they had been invited to celebrate the birth of his brother's son. When I came to pay the bill Ram Bahadur went very pale, and no wonder: he had charged his considerable consumption of rakshi to my account. This made me very angry, and I used some rich Nepali vocabulary I had learned in Kathmandu with just this sort of contingency in mind. The time seemed right to start carrying my own luggage again, and poor Ram Bahadur was paid his wages and summarily dismissed.

Diary, 1 November 1982
A hillside above Manang – about 12,000 feet. Sun setting, ground already frozen; fingers a little numb with cold. To the south my view is completely blocked by Gangapurna towering right overhead. To the north,

behind me, are the only slightly less daunting slopes of Chulu. On my left some yaks are grazing, and beyond them I can see the blue and white prayer flags of the *gompa*, the village monastery, where the lama of Manang blesses travellers (for ten rupees). Away to my right I can just make out the steep valley leading to Tilicho Tal: the 'Great Ice Lake' of Maurice Herzog's epic reconnaissance of the Annapurnas thirty years ago.

In Herzog's day few outsiders had ever visited this valley. How different it is now! In the village European, American and Australian voices vie with the native ones – which may themselves belong to guides or porters from the other side of the country. Among the Manangba people homespun clothes are still the usual form of dress, but for the Nepalese accompanying the trekking parties it seems that tracksuits and down jackets are now *de rigueur*. Combined with the brightly coloured survival gear of the parties themselves, the effect is startling. Happily, among these thirty- or forty-strong groups a few trekkers may still be found doing the circuit on their own. They are sometimes difficult to spot, because they blend into the surroundings like salamanders. I don't mean that they try to pass themselves off as Nepalese – simply that they talk more quietly, wear softer colours and keep their wealth more tactfully hidden than their compatriots. They rarely complain and I get the impression they are more at peace with the country they are passing through. The country is certainly more at peace with them.

I'm making the most of my few days' rest in Manang, because the next part of the circuit will almost certainly be the most difficult. The Thorung La pass leads through the Muktinath Himal at just over 17,500 feet. You need clear weather to cross it, but it's the only way forward to the Thak Khola, and then, eventually, to Pokhara. Considering the state of my health I should perhaps invest in a blessing from the lama. Maybe it will work better than Lomotil.

Manang was the last village of any significance before the Thorung La. It was also the last place I ever saw Wendy and George. I met them coming down as I was going up. George was in the lead, and he was frowning. 'There's deep snow on the pass,' he said. 'We tried to get over but had to give up. It's bloody difficult climbing at this altitude.' He looked back up from where they had come. 'Damn it,' he muttered, and carried on.

Wendy arrived a couple of minutes later. 'How's he taking it?' she asked anxiously.

'Oh, so-so. I think he must be hungry.'

She looked at me conspiratorially. 'The pass isn't that bad really. There's a campsite with water at the foot of the steep bit, just after you leave the river. I'm sure you'll make it if you just take it slowly. Good luck.' And she trudged on after the receding George.

I had come in a great arc around the Annapurna range, and was now in their rain shadow. It was very dry. The soil supported only some miserable potato fields and grazing was limited to skinny horses and a few yaks. On the far side of the valley I thought I spotted some *naaur* or wild blue sheep, but I may have been wrong; these timid animals spend most of their lives on the very edge of the snowline, and are rarely seen. I stood for a while, gazing up at the 25,000 foot ice-peak of Annapurna III directly opposite. A mountain among mountains.

Wendy was right, the pass wasn't that bad, and after camping where she had suggested I reached the 17,500 foot summit the next day with the sun still high in the sky. Behind me Gundang, Chulu and half a dozen other peaks displayed their rosy afternoon colours; ahead was the mountain desert of Mustang.

Mustang occupies a strange niche in the history of Nepal. Much of it was once part of Tibet, and even today many of its inhabitants lead a nomadic life, half in Tibet and half in Nepal. Geographically too, it has more in common with the vast plateau to the north. To approach it from the south one has either to cross the Thorung La as I had done, or to follow the Thak Khola, a river which traverses the Himalaya through the deepest gorge on earth. The upper reaches of this gorge are battered all the year round by high winds; thus for generations the people of Mustang have lived and died in isolation from the outside world.

All this changed in 1959 when China occupied Tibet. Thousands of Tibetans, including the Dalai Lama himself, escaped to Nepal, Sikkim, Bhutan or India, and a few of them organised guerrilla movements against the invading force. Prime movers amongst these were the Kham-pa, a group of nomadic tribes who made their bases in Mustang and Dolpo and were so successful in their gunrunning that in 1974 the Nepalese Army was dispatched to stamp them out. The story of this ruthless 'task force' will probably never be told. The area was immediately closed to foreigners and much of it remains so today. Many of the Kham-pa fought to their deaths, and those who survived were resettled in other parts of Nepal. The saddest thing of all was that just a few years later, in Afghanistan, the episode was enacted all over again, with the Soviet Union taking the place of China and the Mujaheddin taking the place of the Kham-pa tribes – which shows not only that history does repeat itself, but that human beings never learn.

Coming down from the Thorung La, I stumbled upon the shrine of Muktinath almost by mistake. Hidden in a small poplar grove, it was very easy to miss, which would have been a shame because it is one of the most important Hindu pilgrimage sites in the world. I don't suppose the pilgrims have any trouble finding it, because being sensible folk they approach it from the valley below rather than sailing down from the snowy wastes as I did. After slogging up the Thak Khola with its gale force winds, you can bet they have their eyes peeled. The shrine is dedicated to Vishnu the Preserver, a popular Hindu god who appears in many forms including Krishna and, oddly enough, the Buddha. This may explain why Buddhists I met also spoke about Muktinath in reverential tones. The Hindu pilgrims bathe under each of the 108 carved waterspouts fed by some natural springs that rise

under the trees – a brave gesture as the water is ice cold. The
Buddhists are much more practical and direct their rituals
towards a flame that burns from natural gas emerging from a
rock nearby.

Sadly not all the pilgrims I met at Muktinath were looking
for divine inspiration. Most were content to shoot off a few
rolls of Kodachrome, complain that it was colder than Mil-
waukee in January and scamper back down to the hotels in the
valley. They were well groomed, and made me feel like a hobo
down from the mountains – which was exactly what I was. I
pretended not to understand what they were saying and
walked along on tiptoe behind one group, downwind, ears
flapping. It seemed they had flown into Jomosom by special
charter (what did I tell you?) and were on a tour of great
religious sites of the world. Twenty-one faiths in twenty-one
days. Salvation at no extra charge. Next stop Mecca.

From Muktinath the path was wide enough to walk four
abreast. Tea-houses and inns abounded, reminding me that I
was now in the land of the Thakali – people famous
throughout Nepal for their hospitality and commercial drive.
There were a few Tibetan innkeepers too; at least they looked
Tibetan, although their full names written over the doors
invariably included a Hindu component like Gurung or
Bahadur. This mystified me. It was only when I reached
Jomosom that I learned it was a ploy to help them gain social
acceptance and a little more status. In the 1960s it had had a
practical purpose too, because the high school at Jomosom, in
a brief bout of religious zeal, decided it would allow only
Hindu names on its school register.

The Thakali inns reached a new peak in culinary skills,
outstripping even 'K.C.'s' and 'Eat at Joe's'. Their proximity
to Tibet was reflected in their menus by dishes like *foo yung*,
spring roll and a regular but mysterious item called 'Tibetan
bread'. This, I discovered, was a thick disc of unleavened
buckwheat dough the size of a dinner plate – occasionally
fried, but more often just grilled on a hotplate, chapati-style.
Served up at breakfast time, it could be relied upon to keep

one going right through the day. In taste it resembled card-
board: like sitting down to a bowl of cornflakes and then
eating the box as well.

In huge sweeps the path descended 3,000 feet to join the
valley of the Thak Khola. Without warning the wind hit me,
and I understood why this route had such a notorious reputation for bad weather. It came continuously, not in gusts, and
was so strong that for minutes at a time I would stand
motionless, putting all my effort into just bracing myself and
staying upright. Even the birds could make no headway
against it. They flew inches above the ground, heads down,
and as often as not going backwards. Flying sand stung my
face. Bands of horsemen galloped by towards the north,
saluting gravely as if they well understood my problem. I
saluted back as best I could; it was nice to have their sympathy, though I confess I would rather have had their horses.

At Tukche I gave up the unequal struggle and fell, literally,
into an inn. Tukche is a very old town, a stopover point or
caravanserai since Marco Polo's time, where porters, horses
and yaks laden with salt and wool from the north handed over
their goods to people from the south in exchange for grains
and, more recently, manufactured items like soap and candles.
Its single cobbled street was lined with substantial houses with
courtyards for the pack animals and large rooms for storing
their loads. After China occupied Tibet Tukche's traditional
trade went into decline, so the ever-enterprising Thakalis
threw their energy into catering for trekkers. It was cordon
bleu fare. I feasted on noodles followed by, of all things, *crème
caramel*. Escoffier would have turned in his grave.

From Tukche onwards the wind subsided, but the numbers of
trekkers increased until they became a flood. As with the
wind, I put my head down and tried to ignore them. On the
trail this was easy enough because our attentions were
directed to the daily battle with topography and elements;
everybody tended to become lost in their own thoughts. But
my evening visits to inns and tea-houses became increasingly
unpleasant. The air would be filled with shrill voices. 'Where's

the drinking chocolate I ordered ten minutes ago?' 'This hotel's a rip-off.' 'My omelette's cold!' As I neared Pokhara and the end of my dummy run it became steadily worse. If this was what they called civilisation, I decided, it was not for me! I started sleeping in my tent, calling at the tea-houses only to stock up on rice and snatch a quick cup of tea. I was really amazed by the rudeness and thoughtlessness of some trekkers, not only towards local people but even to their own porters. It was hardly surprising that porters had acquired a reputation for abandoning their parties at inconvenient places like the tops of high passes.

Still pondering these cheerless thoughts, I reached the river known as the Modi Khola which drains the legendary Annapurna Sanctuary – a natural amphitheatre eight miles across, whose floor is 14,000 feet above sea level and whose rim includes some of the highest mountains on earth. I stomped into the Sanctuary, still grumpy. It was stunning. From Hiunchuli to the south-west I could turn clockwise and make out Fang, Roc Noir, Gangapurna, three of the Annapurnas (I, III and Annapurna South) and finally the distinctive fish-tailed shape of the sacred Machhapuchhre. Every one of these peaks was higher than any in the continents of Africa, Australia, North America or Europe. Glaciers tumbled off their lower slopes and swept across the Sanctuary floor to where the Modi Khola entered its gorge. My spirits lifted; surely not even whingeing trekkers could intrude on the majesty of this place? I should have known better. Tucked away behind a moraine was a hotel advertising tea, biscuits and pancakes with peanut butter. In the snow beyond, a dozen or so Dayglo tents flapped gently in the afternoon breeze. 'Hi there!' called a familiar Nebraskan voice. 'What kept you?'

This was the last straw. I exploded without warning, hurling all my pent-up anger with the trekkers I had met at this harmless affable man. I swore, I raged, I stamped my boots on the hard-packed snow. He was speechless for a moment, then muttered his apologies and fled to his tent. Perhaps he put my behaviour down to the altitude, or perhaps he thought all English people were like that. I didn't wait to find out. I realised that I had been too long on the well-trodden paths for my own good. The dummy run had served its purpose: I was now as fit as I would ever be, and had learned the basic rules of trekking. It was obviously time to head for the wilderness – to start the walk itself. I covered the thirty remaining miles to Pokhara at full tilt, and quickly found a bus to take me back to Kathmandu. It was 15 November and the Himalayan winter would soon be upon me. I started my preparations immediately, hoping I hadn't left it too late.

4

Kali Gandaki

'I travel not to go anywhere, but to go.'
Robert Louis Stevenson,
Travels with a Donkey in the Cevennes

Three small problems stopped me starting out at once. The first was my grasp of the Nepali language, which I had discovered on the Annapurna Circuit was more or less nil. Around Annapurna this hadn't particularly mattered, as almost everybody knew a little English and was eager to demonstrate it. In north-west Nepal, where I was going, I would find hardly anyone who understood English, let alone my deviant Yorkshire version of it. I would have to learn sufficient Nepali to ask for food and directions – and hopefully a few other things too. My second problem was that there seemed to be no published maps of north-west Nepal. I had a nightmare vision of walking round in circles in the uncharted topography for ever. The third problem was that my one-month visa, the absolute maximum I had been able to get in London, had just run out. So there I was, an illegal immigrant, asking all and sundry in a strange tongue for maps of a remote part of the country where nobody ever went. I should have been arrested.

In Kathmandu, autumn had turned perceptibly to winter. The nights were now cold and starry, the mornings thick with bone-chilling mist. When the sun broke through, usually about 10 am, the days became crisp and clear – in fact just like winter days should be, I reflected, as I trudged the streets in search of a solution to problem number one.

The British Council did offer courses in Nepali, but they

were all booked up; they sent me to the VSO office. VSO provided their language training through the Peace Corps office; they sent me there. The Peace Corps' courses had finished for the year; they sent me to the United Mission to Nepal. I set out for the UMN's language school ...

I found it, with some difficulty, down a muddy lane among the poinsettias, bamboo and banana plants of Thapathali, one of Kathmandu's southern suburbs. The sounds of irregular verbs being conjugated came drifting down from an open window. They were being conjugated very slowly, and I was immediately encouraged; the class seemed just about my level. I walked into the building and knocked on the door marked 'Principal'. '*Hajur*,' said a voice. My confidence evaporated. Did this mean 'Come in' or 'Wait'? I took a chance and opened the door.

The principal, a tall Nepalese, rose from behind his desk and extended his hand warmly. This was a good start: I had obviously translated *hajur* right. 'What can I do for you?'

'I'd like to learn some Nepali, please.'

'Well, yes, I think we can manage that. We run six-month, one-year and two-year courses. How long did you have in mind?'

'Actually I was thinking of a fortnight.'

A frown flickered across the principal's face. 'Ah.' He reflected for a moment. 'Then we will have to give you the Crash Course.'

The Crash Course consisted of seven hours a day of the hardest work I have done since I last attempted O-level Chemistry. My tutors were ruthless; they gave me a really bad time. They also gave me homework. In between lessons I would sit in the school's library and try to study, only to find myself constantly distracted by the sublime views through the window. The poplars around the school had turned golden brown and were decorating the lanes and gardens with their fallen leaves. In the distance, along the northern horizon, the highest peaks of the Himalaya danced in the haze. I had to work late into the night to make up for these hours lost daydreaming – reading by candlelight when Kathmandu's precarious power supply broke down, which it usually did about 7 pm.

During this fortnight I also made game assaults on problems two and three. Problem two – finding a map – turned out to be the easier of the two. Towards the end of the last century the Survey of India organised some clandestine forays into Nepal to survey the country, presumably in the hope that it would one day become part of India. With their dumpy levels concealed beneath their robes, the surveyors travelled the length and breadth of the country, taking bearings and shooting the sun. Their results, though perhaps not quite up to Ordnance Survey or USGS standards, are still the best available for the more remote areas. Actually 'available' isn't quite the word because they are kept strictly under lock and key. But an enterprising individual trading under the name of *Ammonia Print* had somehow secured some hand-drawn copies, which he reproduced by dyeline and sold from a second floor room in a back street of Kathmandu. They weren't exactly detailed maps: more the Nepalese equivalent of a road atlas. But it was comforting to see the names of the places I would be walking through spelt out in black and white – even if, as it turned out, they were mostly wrong.

Problem number three, my lack of papers, was not so simply solved. Nepal's present visa regulations date from the time when officials first noticed a strange type of tourist on the streets. These tourists wore jeans, long hair, bells and beads, and didn't look like tourists at all. They didn't spend money like tourists; they didn't even behave like tourists, apparently preferring to lounge around in the cafés of Kathmandu or by the lakeside at Pokhara with glazed expressions on their faces. Most alarming of all, they were doing this in increasing numbers and often for months on end. Not fully understanding the phenomenon, but with a vague notion that it was not altogether healthy, King Birendra's government decided to ban marijuana and hashish which by tradition had always been freely cultivated and smoked in the hills. At the same time the government imposed strict visa requirements on foreign visitors, and created a special branch of the police to enforce them. I wasn't sure how these police would look upon my expired visa, especially as I would be asking the same police for permission to stay in Nepal for another three months. I approached the Central Immigration Office quaking a little.

The officer in charge took not the slightest notice of my expired visa; in fact it took over an hour to get him to take any notice of me at all.

'You must apply for your extension through the proper channels, sahib.'

'What are they?'

'First you must go to the Director-General of the Department of Tourism. You will present him with your application, your supporting documents and a letter setting out your reasons for wishing to stay in Nepal. The Director-General will consider your case. If your papers are in order, he will recommend the Ministry of Home Affairs to make the necessary authorisation. The Ministry will check their files to make sure you are not *persona non grata*. They will then authorise me to issue you with a special visa. Without this authorisation I can do nothing.'

'How long does that usually take?'

'About two months.'

I felt like a planning applicant who has just had the council's committee procedure explained to him. First, you think they must be joking. Then you say, well, perhaps they were exaggerating the difficulties because it couldn't possibly take that long. Finally, you realise that in fact they were *understating* the complications to soften the blow. At this point planning applicants usually give up the idea, withdraw their application and go in for a less harrowing occupation, like bullfighting. But I needed the visa and I needed it quickly, before the snows came to the high passes. I decided to try a personal approach. I found the Department of Tourism, walked past the glossy posters in the foyer and asked for the Director-General himself.

'I'm sorry, sahib, he is at an international tourism conference in Paris.'

'His deputy, then.'

'He is at a meeting of travel agents in Delhi.'

'His assistant deputy, then.'

'He is inaugurating a new hotel in Kakarbhitta.'

'His assistant deputy's secretary?'

'He is at lunch.'

I made myself at home on the doorstep. The hours crept by. People came and went, and each time I asked the man at the desk if he or she was someone who might possibly deal with my case.

'No, sahib. Be patient. The person you want is Mr Thapa and he is at lunch.'

Mr Thapa arrived at half past four looking tired. I moved quickly, because the office closed at five and I was afraid he might slip away early after his long day. I presented him with my carefully prepared papers and my passport. He looked at them all for a long time, especially the passport which I noticed he was holding upside down. He shifted uncomfortably in his seat as if his lunch was troubling him. 'I will have to show these to the Director-General.'

'But he's in Paris.'

'Ah yes, so he is. Then I will show them to the deputy Director-General.' A thin smile. 'He deals with things in the Director-General's absence, you know.'

'But he's in Delhi.'

Mr Thapa looked even more uncomfortable. 'He is indeed. Thank you for reminding me.' He consulted an impressive looking wallchart. 'In that case I will show them to the assistant deputy.'

'He's gone to Kakarbhitta.'

He looked startled. 'Oh, has he really?'

'Can you authorise my visa?' I asked in desperation.

'Possibly.' He looked at his watch. 'But not today. The office will be closing in five minutes. Can you come back tomorrow?'

It was a harrowing fortnight for Mr Thapa. Each morning I was waiting outside his office, and each afternoon he asked me to come back the following day. But on the Friday of the second week I had a stroke of luck: the Director-General returned from Paris. He agreed to see me and within five minutes had given instructions for my letter of recommendation to be written to the Ministry of Home Affairs. A courier was called to take the letter, and me, direct to its recipient. The courier called it the 'Home Ministry' which made me fear he might be taking me to the Ministry of Housing, but I was reassured as we arrived to see it swarming with policemen and soon found myself, rather to my surprise, facing a door marked 'VISAS'.

What the Director-General's letter said I never knew, because it was written in Devanagari script. But I did notice that it opened many doors for me, and this was the first. After my fortnight with Mr Thapa the efficiency of the uniformed gentleman behind the door was startling. He rattled off some instructions to his assistant, then picked up a telephone – yes, a telephone – and told the Central Immigration Office that Sahib 'Chon' Pilkington would be there in ten minutes with his passport. Would they please give him a three-month special visa, a trekking permit and the booklet about things to do in Kathmandu. He put down the phone, stood to attention and saluted. 'Your papers are awaiting you, sahib. The courier will take you to the Central Immigration Office to collect them.'

I stammered my gratitude, saluted in return and stumbled out of the door. As I followed the courier to the Central Immigration Office I reflected that I wouldn't be needing the booklet about things to do in Kathmandu. I intended to leave the next morning at first light.

The road west from Kathmandu ends after 150 miles, just beyond Pokhara, by the side of a lake. This lake, Phewa Tal, marks the termination of motor cars, electricity, hospitals, pizza – in fact all the elements of civilised life. Beyond Phewa Tal you enter another century, and you, of course, enter it on foot.

West Nepal is dissected by six great rivers: the Kali Gandaki, the Bheri, the Karnali, the Budi Ganga, the Seti and the Mahakali. With their tributaries these six rivers drain 50,000 of the most rugged square miles on earth. To see what Nepal had been like before it was touched by the outside world, I should have to go into the heart of this area, where communications were paths sometimes no more than a foot wide, and the nearest town might be two weeks' walk away. I looked at my dyeline map and decided to head for a great lake which appeared to feed one of the headwaters of the Karnali. The lake was only 10,000 feet above sea level so should still be accessible in late December, when I hoped to arrive. It was called RaRa Tal.

RaRa Tal not only has a strange name but also a strange origin, if legend is to be believed. It is fed from springs 1,800 feet below the surface, and was originally the source of a tributary to the Mugu Karnali which flowed from an outlet on its eastern shore. One day, before the dawn of history, a god called Thakur changed all this. Thakur was a powerful god in more ways than one. With his huge hands he built a dam of earth across the eastern outlet, completely blocking it, and with his huge feet he compacted the earth so hard that his

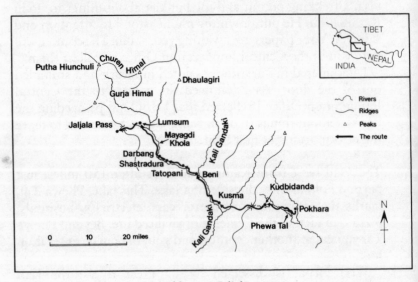

3   Pokhara to Jaljala

footprints can still be seen. Then he fired an arrow from his giant bow and opened the present outlet to the Khatyar Khola on the other side of the lake. It was prehistoric civil engineering at its best.

To get to RaRa Tal I would have to walk across the basins of two of the six rivers, the Kali Gandaki and the Bheri, and partly across that of the Karnali which was the third. I would try to return to civilisation via the remainder of the Karnali basin and then across the Budi Ganga and Seti to the Mahakali which forms Nepal's western frontier with India. The few people I had met who were familiar with west Nepal had reckoned that the first part of the journey would take about five weeks – if I was lucky with the weather and didn't encounter any blocked passes. The second part was a different matter altogether. The Seti, Budi Ganga and Mahakali seemed to be rivers that no one in Kathmandu had heard of.

I found a truck going to Pokhara – one of those Indian-built ones that so endearingly say TATA on the back. I thought this might be safer than taking the bus. I was right: the laden truck crawled along so slowly that I found myself almost hoping for a minor mishap just to liven things up. As if in answer to my thoughts, the driveshaft broke. Incredibly, the driver and his mechanic managed to repair it, more or less, in a mere two hours while the half dozen passengers we had picked up along the way stood around and made helpful suggestions. We chugged into Pokhara at ten miles per hour just after dark. I walked to where the tarmac petered out at the lake and booked myself into one of the lakeside lodges. It felt like the end of the known world.

Next morning I awoke with a lump in my throat. The lump grew while I showered in the lodge's corrugated iron outhouse; it grew while I dressed; and it grew while I faced my last Western-style breakfast, unable to eat. Machhapuchhre shimmered on the northern horizon, magnificent and mocking. The lump was still there as I left the lodge, left the tarmac with its noisy buses and trucks, left the tourist restaurants clustered along the lake's eastern shore, left the whole 'civilised' world and struck out along the lakeside footpath heading west. And then, like magic, it was gone.

The path hugged the lakeshore round its many headlands, and wound through muddy paddy-fields where the lake formed inlets in the tributary valleys. The rice harvest was in full swing, and the hillsides were alive with activity and the sounds of voices shouting and singing. The jobs of reaping and carrying in the rice from the fields belonged to the women and children, and they came in droves along the path, bundles strapped to their backs so that from behind they looked like walking haystacks, with just their feet sticking out at the bottom. Threshing was done in the villages, either by the men who would beat the stems of rice on the ground until the grain fell off, or by teams of oxen which would be made to walk in circles, stamping the stems with their hooves. Then the older women took over, winnowing the grain by sieving it through wicker dishes, and laying it out on roofs and in courtyards to form golden carpets, drying in the sun. At this time of the year the roofs were already laden with a variety of colourful produce set out to ripen – yellow maize cobs, bright green peppers and great orange pumpkins – so that many villages took on the appearance of a bazaar.

Harvesting was an operation in which everyone played a part, and the enthusiasm with which each member of the family contributed to this medieval-style production line was infectious. They waved and shouted greetings which I was astonished to find I understood. '*Namaste saathi! Tapaaiko desh kun ho? Kahaa jaane?* Good morning, friend! Where do you come from? Where are you going?'

'*Mero desh England ho, RaRa Tal-maa jaanchhu,*' I cried, 'I come from England and I'm off to RaRa Tal!' The words had a nice ring and I found myself saying them proudly, almost believing them. *I come from England and I'm off to RaRa Tal.*

The path left the lake and came to a fork in the valley which wasn't marked on my map. I approached an old woman washing clothes. '*Kusma-maa jaane baato kun ho?*' I recited hesitantly, 'Which way is it to Kusma please?'

The woman gabbled, waving her arms in all directions. '*Yo baato Kusma-maa jaanchha; tyo pani. Ekai hun.*' She spoke in a strange accent, not at all like my teacher in Kathmandu. I couldn't understand a word. Despondently, I thanked her and carried on.

Coming down the path was an old man in a faded military uniform. I repeated the question: '*Kusma-maa jaane baato kun ho?*'

The man waved his arms. '*Yo baato Kusma-maa jaanchha; tyo ...*' He stopped in mid-sentence as he sensed my incomprehension, then lowered his voice conspiratorially. 'Do you speak English?' he asked.

If proof were needed that old soldiers never die, this uniformed veteran provided it. He had been a Gurkha, he announced proudly: a captain in the famous brigade of Nepalese soldiers. After a life of active service in India, Hong Kong and Britain, he was now drawing a pension and living out his days in the valley where he had been born. He said he had fought in both World Wars, and I could believe him, because he looked at least 100 years old. 'Tell me,' he asked. 'How is Aldershot these days?'

What the woman washing clothes had apparently been trying to tell me was that I could take either of the two forks; they both led to Kusma, the administrative centre of the Parbat district, which was the next significant place on my map. 'If you take the left one you can stay at my house,' said the captain.

We climbed the zigzag path together – the captain stepping lightly, me gasping for breath. On the steeper slopes the paddy-fields were like giant steps carved out of the hillside, the walls between one terrace and the next as high as the terraces themselves were wide. A woman carrying an enormous bundle of straw on her back set it down to rest for a moment and it toppled over, tossing and turning down the hill. She chased after it with easy strides, laughing. I shared her *joie de vivre* but not, alas, her energy. By the time we had climbed to the captain's village of Kudbidanda, 3,000 feet above Phewa Tal, I was done for.

We found the captain's house in the shade of an ancient pipal tree overlooking the village green. It was a village of the Gurung people, easily identifiable by the distinctive orange and ochre painted mud walls of its houses, and their over-hanging thatched roofs. The captain's house was noticeably more substantial than the rest. It was built of rough-hewn slabs of stone: paid for, he assured me, by his army pension of 400 rupees a month.

He ushered me on to his verandah and pulled up two chairs. 'I think you must be a little tired, and probably hungry too. My daughter is already making tea. Later we will have some daal bhaat, yes?' I nodded vigorously and smiled in return. I was beginning to like this man.

The Gurkhas – a brigade of regiments of the British and Indian Armies with a history going back 170 years – take their name rather curiously from a small district of central Nepal from which only a few Gurkha soldiers come nowadays. At the beginning of the nineteenth century the King of Gorkha, Prithwi Narayan, built up a tremendous armed force from among the Gurung and Magar people of this area and embarked on a series of conquests across the whole Himalaya from Kashmir to Bhutan. The British, who also had territorial claims here, declared war, and in the bitter ensuing campaign the reputation of the 'Gorkhas', or Gurkhas, was sealed. They fought with a courage and tenacity never before witnessed by the British officers. Thousands died, but when peace came in 1816 the British (who knew a good thing when they saw it) took their former enemies into their own service. Four bat-talions were raised immediately, and others followed until by the time of the Second World War they included close on a quarter of a million men.

Recruitment has never been much of a problem. Every year a small band of recruiting officers (many of them retired NCOs like my host) march off into the mountains with orders to bring back sixty-seven men. Inducements are not necessary; they are beseiged by volunteers wherever they go. For most Nepalese people, army service offers a much better life than they could ever hope for in their own village – not to mention social standing and the all-important pension, brought round by the Gurkha paymaster on an annual pilgrimage which lasts two and a half months. After a first round of selection at staging posts in the hills, about twice the number required are taken to the main recruiting depots at Pokhara and Dharan, where further tests root out the final lucky few. In some years there are as many as 300 applicants for every place.

We sipped our tea. The shadow of the pipal tree lengthened, and the stones of the house behind us glowed warmly in the evening sun. The captain disappeared indoors and returned carrying a three foot long khukri, the Nepalese knife which achieved immortality as the Gurkhas' weapon in campaigns from the Indian Mutiny to the Falklands War. Its bone handle was carved into the shape of an animal's head – mouth open, teeth bared and tongue protruding belligerently. The captain pulled the implement from its scabbard and offered it proudly for me to examine its curved razor-sharp blade; then, in a savage swoop, he showed how a soldier could use the notch at the base of the blade to twist a weapon out of an enemy's hand.

From the age of about twelve most Nepalese carry a khukri in their belts. They are all-purpose tools, equally fit for reaping crops, scything grass, cutting foliage and firewood, butchering animals, peeling vegetables or cleaning one's toe-nails. Few are as elaborate as the battle-scarred one I was now turning over in my hands; most are beaten out from old car springs or lengths of railway line.

I commented on the many stories I had heard of the Gurkhas' bravery – a quality which has earned them no fewer than twenty-six Victoria Crosses. 'Yes,' said my host, 'our motto is *Kaaphar hunu bhandaa marnu raamro*: It is better to die than to be a coward. Quite a few of my friends were called upon to act on that motto, and they never failed to do so.'

As we talked, the children of Kudbidanda stopped their playing and trotted up one by one. Wide-eyed and open-mouthed, they gathered in a semicircle, blotting out the last of the remaining light. They listened intently to our strange words, occasionally whispering to each other, but mostly silent except for their noses. Nepalese children have congenital runny noses – possibly a Himalayan version of hay fever. Unfortunately they don't have a great sense of etiquette, and Kleenex has yet to invade their lives. So they control the flow by good old-fashioned sniffing, which they do unashamedly, continually, very loudly and apparently to good effect. From where I sat in the middle of the semicircle it came over in pure stereo, like the BBC Symphony Orchestra tuning up for the last night of the Proms.

Supper was brought in by another of my host's daughters (old enough, like the first, to be my grandmother, though I thought it better not to say so). As the sun slipped behind the hillside opposite we rinsed our hands in the bowls of water offered and plunged them into the steaming rice. The daughter who had served the meal waited just long enough to hear my murmurs of approval, then melted back indoors. I asked if the family ever ate together, but my host looked so shocked by this outrageous idea that I hastily returned to our previous subject.

I had often heard of the intense rivalry between Gurkha regiments, and recalled a story about the First World War which seemed appropriate to my present male company. It concerned a battalion stationed on the Suez Canal. In Nepal, the greatest insult a man can direct at another is to expose himself to him, and this battalion found themselves in a position to show their contempt for their colleagues in other regiments in a novel and effective way. Every time a troopship passed by with a particularly despised Gurkha unit on board, they would be greeted by the astonishing spectacle of dozens of men rushing down to the bank waving their genitalia. Was there any truth in this unlikely story, I asked. 'Oh yes,' replied my host, 'I was one of them.'

Next morning, a little overawed by the enormous distance I had to cover, I decided that progress was more important than breakfast. The whole village turned out to watch me go: the children running alongside, the grown-ups waving from the village green until I passed out of sight behind a bluff. I walked briskly for an hour, invigorated by their prodigious hospitality, and arrived quite unexpectedly at the next village. There, to my astonishment, I found another man in faded military uniform beckoning me to another verandah where another two stools had been set out, with breakfast on a table in between. By some extraordinary means the word had travelled ahead of me, not only of my approach but of my breakfastlessness as well. I sat down, speechless, to an extraordinary meal of rice cakes, rice spaghetti, a fried egg and a glass of buffalo milk. 'Pleased to make your acquaintance,' said the old soldier as he sat down opposite me. 'Do you by any chance know a place called Aldershot?'

Fuelled by rice cakes and buffalo milk, I climbed a magnificent stone staircase to the first pass. Beyond, the Kali Gandaki beckoned mistily from its gorge a mile below. Kusma lay somewhere in the gorge, and in Kusma, hopefully, my next night's sleep.

As I walked west, I passed dozens of porters heading east towards Pokhara with goods for the city markets. They walked painfully, bent almost double under dokos piled high above their heads. Most were Pun Magar people from the upper valleys of the Kali Gandaki's tributaries. Some, I knew, would be walking for five days to sell their miserable loads of rice, cornflour or rancid butter, and would then face a walk of five days home again. I found it difficult to believe that such an arduous journey would be worth the paltry sum they would receive, if they were lucky, in the markets. But, of course, this was just my Western mentality; to the Pun Magars, the Pokhara bazaars were an obvious and lucrative way of converting their surplus produce into hard cash.

Approaching Kusma at dusk, I ran into a boy with a worried brow. He introduced himself as Lal Bahadur and showed me what was bothering him. '*General Matriculation Part Two*' said the paper, '*Intermediate English*'. Poor Lal Bahadur had spent his day in an examination room, doing comprehensions and trying not to split his infinitives. Having just suffered two weeks of the same thing in Nepali, I could understand his difficulty. He was sure he had failed, he said;

English was so *murkha*. I looked this up in my dictionary and found it meant 'stupid'. I told him I thoroughly agreed; I found it just as much of a struggle as he did. I don't think it was quite the right thing to say. He looked very taken aback, excused himself and wandered away looking even more worried than before.

This was the night of the full moon, and when it rose over the eastern mountains the dogs of Kusma went beserk. Canine emotions reached new heights. All night they howled, a hundred Hounds of the Baskervilles baying to each other across the hills. Neither they, I, nor I suspect any of the inhabitants of the neatly whitewashed houses of Kusma got so much as a wink of sleep.

Three days out from Pokhara, my walking was already begin-ning to fall into a pattern. Each morning I would put a respectable distance behind me, then stop for a mid-morning breakfast as the Nepalese do. This would consist of rice cakes (sometimes dyed horrible shades of pink or green) or the by now familiar daal bhaat – rice and lentils. With the first meal of the day inside me, I would then tackle the path more energetically and often covered most of the day's distance before the call of the tea-houses would draw me back again in the mid-afternoon heat. Tea and biscuits would keep me going until nightfall and the irresistible smell of supper at a village *bhaati* or inn. Supper would be (you guessed) daal bhaat, with some green vegetables or tarkaari – usually soggy cabbage – if I was lucky. A little after-dinner conversation (rather limited by my appalling difficulties with the local accent), a little reflecting on the day's progress, then I would crawl into my sleeping bag in a corner of the room and drift gently off to sleep, my dreams always accompanied by the thud, thud, thud of my boots on the mountain path. This idyllic way of life would come to an end when I crossed the Jaljala pass and entered the catchment of the Bheri. Then there would be no more tea-houses; I would be on my own.

On this third day I dispensed with my watch. Like my camera it was a dreadful intrusion – impossible to disguise and attracting the hawk-eyed gaze of everybody I met. 'Plee-as what tiy-am is it?' was not a question I could ignore, even though to me time had by now lost its meaning. So I stuffed the watch and all its irrelevant hours and minutes into the bottom of my pack. The sun would tell me all I needed to know, and without having to be wound up.

Following the path up the Kali Gandaki towards the bazaar town of Beni, I remembered the other place of that name that I had approached in a rather similar fashion in 1979. That time the country had been Bolivia and the Beni had been Alto, or Upper, Beni on the eastern slopes of the Andes. On that occasion the heavily forested foothills had been carved into steep ridges and gorges by the headwaters of the Amazon. This Beni, whose waters flowed not to the Amazon but to the Ganga, was similar except that it had many more people. In spite of its chronic shortage of cultivable land, the gorge of the Kali Gandaki was in fact more densely populated than any Andean valley I ever saw – even though just as remote from the towns and cities which are such strong magnets for rural people today. It was an unexpected contrast which I decided to make the most of; Beni was the last place of any significance, geographically speaking, that I would encounter for several weeks.

I found the town perched on a spur between the main river and one of its western tributaries, the Mayagdi Khola. It was abuzz with activity – its single street thronged with noisy animals and people. Shopkeepers proudly displayed their wares of soap, biscuits, candles and what have you, all brought from Pokhara by pack animal, or, more likely, by porter. There were also goods that had come down from Mustang and Tibet by the pony caravans I had met previously on the Thak Khola. I was particularly tempted by an exquisitely embroidered shirt in one shop. 'Yes,' said the shopkeeper, 'It is from Mustang. My brother got it from the traders at Tukche.' After some polite haggling I bought the shirt, looking forward to wearing it beyond RaRa Tal, where I would be back among Tibetans. I sat down in a tea-house and held it up proudly against my chest. The other customers murmured their appreciation. I basked happily in the warmth of their interest and in the beauty of my new acquisition, and on an impulse ordered tea for everyone. Then I happened to turn up the collar. Behind it was a small label; it read, 'WARM WASH. COOL IRON. DO NOT DRY CLEAN.'

Voices hailed me from across the street. 'John! *Bonjour! Ça va?*' I looked up and recognised the French party from Dumre. Three of them came over and sat down. I stared at them, momentarily dumbstruck, then quickly hid my embarrassing shirt and found my tongue.

'Hello! How did you get here?'

'Oh, we came down the Thak Khola from Muktinath and forgot to turn left . . . '

I gasped.

' . . . so we thought we'd walk out to the south.'

'What about your flight home?'

'Two of the girls have gone back to Kathmandu to change the tickets with Air France.'

A thought crossed my mind. 'Gertie and Antoinette?'

'*Oui*, Gertie and Antoinette.'

'Oh.'

The group had filled what few respectable hotels Beni possessed, and I found myself a room in an insalubrious place called the Hotel Good Luck. It backed on to the town's public convenience, which backed on to the river. The hotel's only other occupant was an austere German who introduced herself as Ulrike. At least I think that was what she said. It was almost all she did say; she appeared to be a woman of few words, and after exchanging some monosyllables of greeting we consumed our evening meal in silence. Here, I thought, was a truly independent traveller, avoiding the traps that others set by the simple trick of avoiding others. I remembered Wendy and George, who had chosen companionship and suffered for their choice. Their reasons for coming to Nepal had perhaps been different from Ulrike's, but I couldn't help feeling that of the two ways of travelling, Ulrike's had much to be said for it.

I retired early to a room at the back of the house and was

soon sound asleep, lulled by the muted echo of the river's roar on the far valley side. Some hours later I awoke to pandemonium. From Ulrike's room were coming bumps, bangs and some exceptionally lurid Saxon expletives whose meaning I didn't fully understand, but could guess. She sounded frantic. I leapt out of my sleeping bag, the very epitome of the valiant knight, a little short on shining armour but prepared to do battle all the same. In my drowsiness I caught my toe in the bag's drawcord and fell headlong into a pile of earthenware pots stacked by the door. The crash was deafening but its effect was immediate; the sounds from Ulrike's room stopped as if someone had thrown a switch. First Ulrike's, then the proprietor's head appeared round the door. *'Um Gotteswillen!'* cried Ulrike, 'What *are* you doing?'

I explained lamely that I had been trying to rescue her from what sounded at the very least like attempted rape. For the first time I saw her smile. 'It wasn't necessary, but thanks for the thought,' she ventured, and stumbled back to her room. The proprietor didn't smile. 'What about my pots?' he asked plaintively.

I left Beni early without ceremony or breakfast. A few miles up the Mayagdi Khola, I stepped to one side to let a funeral procession pass. The leaders held aloft a great white sheet on bamboo poles. Then came the pallbearers, supporting the body on a crude bamboo frame covered with an orange shroud. Friends and relatives brought up the rear – about three dozen of them, looking a touch tipsy I thought. They explained that the body belonged to a woman who had drowned in the Mayagdi Khola. I looked at the raging, turbulent stream and tried to imagine what it would be like to die such a violent death. It was a precipitous valley: if I didn't watch carefully where I was putting my feet, maybe I would find out.

A smell of sulphur told me that I was approaching the village of Tatopani. Tatopani means hot springs (literally 'hot water'). There is an abundance of these splendid natural facilities throughout the Himalaya; only fifteen miles to the north-east, a larger village called Tatopani which I had already visited on my dummy run had no less than four, the water carefully channelled into bathing pools where you could resuscitate tired muscles and at the same time ruminate on some of the most spectacular scenery in the world. Hot springs are a magnet for travellers, and I felt privileged to have these on the Mayagdi Khola to myself. The pleasure was doubled by one of the best lunches I had enjoyed for days: a meal of daal bhaat and tarkaari for which I was asked just five rupees – about 22p. As I was leaving the tea-house the old lady asked if I would like to take her daughter with me: a tempting offer, but as her daughter wasn't around to say what she thought of the idea I asked the old lady to come instead. Everybody laughed except the old lady, who shook her head violently. I made my escape before she could change her mind.

In the village of Shastradura the children threw stones at me from a vantage point above the path. I often found myself the target of endearing little gestures like this. Sometimes they would hurl rocks, sometimes clods of earth; whatever they could lay their hands on, I suppose. Their parents would look benignly on their offspring's efforts, as if this was quite a normal and friendly way to greet a stranger. However, on this occasion there were no adults in sight, so I addressed the children myself. From a safe distance I told them they were doing the cause of tourism no good, and were also rotten shots, which they were. They didn't reply, but I noticed that the hail of missiles dried up, and I made my way unmolested to the village of Darbang.

Here the valley narrowed dramatically. Landslides during the previous monsoon had swept away acres of rice paddies on the steeper slopes, and the path picked its way through the debris by the river. A wedding procession passed, looking uncannily like the funeral procession I had encountered earlier. The path climbed in zigzags, beginning its approach to the 11,000 foot Jaljala pass which would lead me to my next great river, the Bheri. On one side of the valley was broadleaf *sal* woodland; on the other side, where less rain fell, grew a forest of sweet-smelling chir pine.

Now that I had left the paths used regularly by trekkers, I was constantly the centre of attention. Whenever I stopped in a village the whole population would invariably gather round to have a look. This gave me plenty of opportunity to practise my Nepali, but it quickly wore me down and I would cherish the moment each evening when I bundled myself into my sleeping bag and was finally left in peace. I didn't really blame people for this regal treatment, considering what a curious apparition I must have been. Where I live we'd probably do just the same in similar circumstances: that is, if suddenly paid a visit by a man from Mars.

As I tramped along, now high up the valley side, a young girl came running up with a stick of sugar-cane. She presented it proudly, then showed me how to split the cane and suck out the delicious juice. We walked along hand in hand for a while. Across the valley came the sound of a flute, played delicately by a shepherd boy whose flock I could just make out in the pastures among the trees. The music grew louder, then softer as it floated on the afternoon breeze.

Two more days brought me to Lumsum and the final approach to the pass. I stopped in the village to restock my groceries. Ten rupees bought a bagful of beans, a handful of sugar and a couple of new laid eggs, plus countless cups of tea, while a woman bartered with me for my plastic bags.

The path wound remorselessly upwards. I climbed for three hours without stopping. The pack chafed my shoulders. I swore at it, but it only chafed more. I passed some alluring false summits, convinced that each would be the final one. It wasn't. As I climbed, I noticed that the streams which crossed the path were no longer of water but of solid ice. Even in the afternoon sunshine the air was bitterly cold. Fortunately it had not snowed recently, and the snow on the ground, although deep, was grey and harmless.

The sal trees and chir pine had by now given way to a forest of oak, hemlock and that most magnificent of Nepal's native trees, the rhododendron. In spring, this astonishing plant bursts into a blossom so spectacular that the Nepalese refer to it as a flower rather than a tree – even though it can reach up to seventy feet in height. For a few weeks of the year its pinks, reds and yellows stand out in superb contrast to the white mountains and the blue sky. Over forty species of rhododendron have been identified, each occupying a narrow band of altitude where the climate suits it best. The ones around me were *Rhododendron arboreum*, the so-called tree rhododendron which has been adopted as Nepal's national flower.

Birds were abundant in the forest, even at this late season. Flocks of choughs swooped noisily above the mantle, their red and yellow beaks visible briefly in the sunlight as they flashed across gaps between the trees. A danphe bird, recognisable by its bright turquoise crest, broke cover with a cackle and soared away across the valley. And for a short time, silent but clearly silhouetted against the sky, the distinctive shape of a golden eagle circled high above me. I was not the only one who spotted it; with a crash of vegetation a pair of Himalayan squirrels ran headlong for cover across my path.

After another hour the forest thinned, the rhododendron gave way to birch and fir, and as the sun dipped in the west I emerged blinking from the trees on to the broad meadow of Jaljala. With dusk came a new problem. I had counted on being able to find water near the pass, but for the last two hours of climbing it had all been frozen. I didn't cherish the prospect of melting snow. In the gathering darkness I started down the other side, eyes and ears strained for signs of running water. There was nothing. Not a drop. Not a drip. Not a rill. Not a gurgle. Not a trickle. I was in a jumble of inert, waterless rocks. I listened intently but was greeted only by my heavy breathing in the rarefied air, and the clang of steel on stone as I prodded my ice-axe through the crust of snow, feeling for a safe footing. I was desperately thirsty, and cursed myself roundly for not having filled the water container earlier.

Sometimes I think I have a protective genie which springs to my rescue at times like this. I had just resigned myself to a parched and miserable night, and was squinting through the blackness for some level snow on which to pitch the tent, when two things happened at once. Out of the shadows on my left appeared the dark shape of a shepherd's hut, and away to my right I heard the sound of a stream. I could hardly believe my luck. I approached the hut and peered through its single tiny window. 'Is anybody there?' No reply. It was deserted. I tottered gratefully in.

In the peacefulness of that lonely evening, all the agony and apprehension of getting there drifted away like ice crystals on the wind. Warmed by a juniper fire and with a good supper inside me, I took my bedtime mug of tea to the hut's porch and sat facing the silent mountains. Directly in front of me Putha Hiunchuli, Churen Himal and Gurja Himal, all over 23,000 feet, caught the last rays of the evening sun. To the right lay Dhaulagiri, the sixth highest peak in the world, looking much closer than its twenty-two miles' distance; then my old friends the Annapurnas; and finally, fifty miles to the east, Machha-puchhre, the fish-tail mountain which had kept me company on my first day out from Pokhara. A three-quarter moon rose over the Kali Gandaki, bathing the meadow in a ghostly white light. Towards the north a wolf howled. I lay back, watched a shooting star, and my bedtime tea went forgotten and cold.

5

Across the Bheri
to Jumla

'I suffered increasingly from mountaineer's
foot – a reluctance to put one in front of the
other.'

H. W. Tilman, *Nepal Himalaya*

My sleep was punctuated with throwing curses at the inhabitants of the hut – a family of fieldmice which spent most of the night noisily investigating my belongings. Whoever conjured up the phrase 'quiet as a mouse' had obviously not come across these. My juniper fire on the porch quickly died, and the freezing cold of the Himalayan night numbed my fingers and toes. I scrambled indoors, bumped my head on the stone lintel, yelped, and buried myself deep in the farthest recesses of the hut. It wasn't just that it was cold; I was frightened of the wolf. In my drowsiness I had fancied I could make out its black shape moving across the snow, green eyes glowering maliciously at me through the darkness. Of course, I may have dreamed it all (which would at least have made a change from dreaming about pizza) but the next morning I spotted wolf-like footprints within twenty yards of the hut.

A fiery sunrise quickly melted much of the snow. I breakfasted on beans, scrambled eggs and the previous night's tea warmed up. In the daylight I could now see that the hut was the sole building in a broad sloping meadow, the beginning of a valley whose surrounding crags, which I could make out clearly ahead of and behind me, were clothed in juniper and fir trees. The crags and trees made intricate patterns in the snow,

72

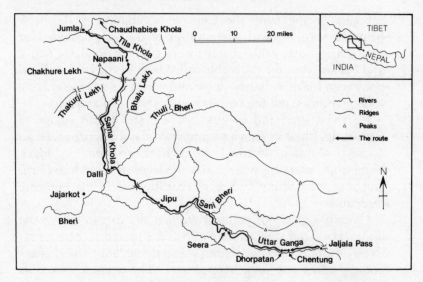

4   Jaljala to Jumla

a lacy patchwork of black, green and white that took me back
to distant days in Yellowstone's back-country. The similarity
was brought home to me when a birdcall from a rock made me
glance round to see the unmistakable shape of a horned lark –
a familiar sight around Old Faithful, where this tame bird
used to vie with the geyser for visitors' affections. This feeling
that I was in another place, on another continent, stayed with
me as I packed my things and trudged down the huge, silent
valley. It was December now, and the *goths*, or seasonal
shepherds' huts, had been boarded up for the winter. I had the
valley and the mountains to myself.

My next destination was Dhorpatan, still 9,300 feet above
sea level but a full day's walk down the valley. When spoken
quickly the name sounds exactly like 'Dolly Parton', so for
days I had delighted in answering the inevitable question
'Where you-a go-eeng?' by declaring, 'I'm going to Dolly
Parton.' Here a tributary of the Bheri called the Uttar Ganga
disgorges into a wide valley, and here in 1959 King Mahen-
dra's government provided sanctuary for some of the 90,000

73

refugees fleeing from the Chinese occupation of Tibet. A beautiful spot, but with a harsh climate, it hardly provided for easy living. Some 800 Tibetans were coaxing potatoes, maize and barley from the miserable soil. Much of the land was too poor even for these hardy crops, and was given over to grazing scraggy horses and the cow-yak hybrid known as a *dzo*.

I arrived tired and hungry in the first Tibetan village of Chentung. I hadn't seen a soul for two days. I approached an ancient woman, swathed from head to foot in black homespun, carrying water from the river in a big brass urn. She saw me coming and went scuttling off in the opposite direction.

I found a group of younger women chatting in one of the doorways. They were similarly attired. I smiled at them tentatively. '*Namaste, khaanekuraa yahaa paainchha?* Good afternoon – can I buy food here please?' The women looked at each other, giggled, scurried inside and slammed the door.

I trudged up and down the dusty street, appealing to the bolted shutters and the deserted doorways. Silence. I peered down side alleys leading to stony vegetable patches. They were empty and infested with weeds. It was like Virginia City at high noon. I felt very drowsy. I put down my pack, propped it against the mud wall of a house, propped myself against the pack and closed my eyes.

Half an hour later I was woken from my slumber by a very small noise close to my right ear. It was the sound of a bolt being drawn. The sound was followed by that of a door moving on a rusty hinge. I didn't open my eyes. There was a short silence, then a shuffling sound and I felt a tap on my shoulder. I looked up to see the ancient woman bending over me, her wrinkled face hidden deep in the folds of her homespun. She beckoned me to come inside, and smiled cryptically as I stared around her home. Like all Tibetan houses, it was black from mud floor to thatched ceiling. All its contents were black: its clay oven, its sparse and spartan furniture and its shelves of cooking utensils lining the walls. The woman, dressed in black, dissolved into the black surroundings. The late afternoon sunshine slanting in through the single window penetrated no more than a couple of feet into the room, but as my eyes grew accustomed to the dark I could see the woman looking calmly at me, not questioning, but still smiling slightly, as if people from Mars dropped by regularly.

I asked if there was any food available. Only this, she said, measuring out some *tsampa*, the coarsely ground and roasted barley flour which Tibetans eat when there is nothing else. She handed a bowlful to me. Misunderstanding, I tried to swallow a little, and choked on the dry powder. '*Dhairya garnus,*' she laughed, 'Be patient,' and set a kettle to heat on the clay oven. When it had boiled she made tea – not Tibetan-style with yak butter, I was glad to see, but in the Indian way with sugar. Still smiling she poured the tea on to the tsampa. Mixed into a thick porridge the flour tasted much better, and didn't make me choke.

In my halting Nepali I asked if she liked living in Dhorpatan. '*Maato raamro ho ra haawaapaani raamro ho,*' she replied, '*Tara maachho chhaina*' – which, if I understood her correctly, meant 'The soil and climate are OK, but I miss the fish.' She went on to tell me that she came from the shores of Nam Tso, a lake beyond the Khalamba La pass north of Lhasa. This may have explained the bit about the fish. The catches from Nam Tso must have been of Galilean proportions, because she went on at some length about them, indicating the size of the creatures with outstretched arms in the way that fishing people do. She may have been exaggerating a little; I know an angler in Hampshire who says that dimensions of prize catches grow in the catcher's memory by 10 per cent with every month that passes. I asked the woman how long it was since she had left Nam Tso. 'Twenty-three years,' she said.

Tsampa propelled, I covered the three miles to the main village at a sprint. Dhorpatan, like its near namesake, covers quite a wide area, but this place was clearly its commercial and spiritual centre. It could be identified from all over the valley by its white and blue prayer flags, fluttering gaily among the fir trees as if announcing the arrival of a circus. Prayer flags are the means by which Buddhists cast their prayers or *mantras* to the four winds. The mantra is printed on the material hundreds or perhaps thousands of times, and is also to be found inscribed on stones and rocks, the intricate Tibetan script painstakingly carved and coloured with bright pigments. I had seen prayer flags and prayer stones elsewhere where Buddhists lived, the flags often tattered with age, the stones covered in lichen. But never so many as here. The flags completely dwarfed the village's wooden monastery; the stones were heaped around it pile upon pile. The condition of the stones was particularly revealing – they were freshly quarried and carved. Their cut faces glistened with the same message repeated again and again:

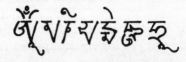

– '*Om mani padme hum*. Hail, jewel in the heart of the lotus.' All the stones had been made in the last twenty years: a seemingly superhuman task which pointed dramatically to the distress felt by these refugees from across the Himalaya – and to the strength of their faith in the Buddha.

Everybody who arrives in Dhorpatan at dusk is taken to Tukden's house. Here the pony trains from the south disembark their loads of rice, sugar and tea, and a constant stream of visitors come in for provisions, other business or just to pass the time of day. Like the one in Chentung, Tukden's house was black from floor to ceiling. Seats and benches lined the walls of the main room, and scattered on these were thick, comfortable Tibetan rugs, each carefully handwoven to an intricate pattern of reds, maroons and blues. They gave an immediate impression of warmth and hospitality, expectations which were quickly fulfilled since Tukden turned out to be an innkeeper of the first order. He happened to be out when I first arrived, but his 'staff' – three Tibetan youths in yakskin waistcoats and boots – had been well

instructed in the art of hotel management. I was offered a
bowl of tea, Tibetan-style this time with no milk or sugar but
with some rather rancid yak butter floating in it. It was very
salty, like Scotch broth; the yak butter was chewy and tasted
of lard. I took a few sips, made some appreciative noises and
discreetly poured what was left through a crack in the wooden
wall. After reassuring myself that nobody had noticed this
shifty behaviour, I set about exploring the rest of the house
while the 'staff' busied themselves preparing supper.

There were only two rooms. The second one was, if possible, even blacker than the first. It was a larder and saddlery
for the whole of Dhorpatan: the place where the pony trains'
loads were stored and their tackle kept. Sacks of grain were
stacked along two walls, some already ground, others not. I
identified *maake* (yellow maize flour) and the tsampa which I
had been given at Chentung. A sack of *chini* – roughly
granulated sugar – was set apart from the rest. Dominating
everything were two enormous brass cauldrons, filled to the
brim with dark mixtures which, to judge by their evil smell,
were in a fairly advanced state of fermentation. I took a ladle
and extracted some liquid from the first; it had once been rice,
but was now well on the way to becoming *chang*, an illicit
home-brewed beer that I had been assured was more potent
even than the deadly Old Peculier they brew in Yorkshire. The
second cauldron contained grains like the barley in the sacks.
This bouillon already smelt like methylated spirit and was
obviously destined to become rakshi, the high-octane fire-
water which had had such a devastating effect on Ram
Bahadur in Chame.

Meanwhile, Tukden himself had arrived home. He was a
small man, surprisingly lean, his skin drawn taut over high
cheekbones with not a trace of the buttery complexion I had
seen in other Tibetan faces. He clasped my hand and welcomed me in his native Tibetan. I do not understand Tibetan
but the meaning was eloquently conveyed in his eyes.

Over a supper of noodles and unleavened bread Tukden
began speaking in Nepali, and told me about some of the
hazards ahead. He described how the Uttar Ganga flowed

through precipitous gorges, banging his fist on the table to simulate the crashing of the water on the rocks. He stretched his arm high above his head, then down to his feet, to indicate how the path climbed to the tops of the highest ridges and then plunged down to join the river in its gorge. He announced gravely that I would find no *baas basnu* (accommodation) and no *khaanekuraa* (food) until I crossed the Thuli Bheri – the Great Bheri – a week's walk away. Tukden was no alarmist, and I took him at his word; I decided to stock up well from his plentiful storeroom before continuing. I suppose his animated warnings should have alerted me to the possibility that there might be other dangers too. But I was drowsy with exhaustion and full of good food, and the last thing I wanted to do was think about tomorrow. I lay back on his rugs and cushions and was instantly asleep.

In the pale light before dawn, I awoke to hear Tudken humming his mantra as he stoked up the fire and set the kettle to boil. *'Om mani padme hummmm, Om mani padme HUMMMM!'* As the sun rose his droning incantation softened to a whisper and he set to work with flour and water, kneading dough to make several rounds of unleavened bread which he served hot with goat's butter and, to my dismay, more Tibetan tea. Before I left I took the two remaining plastic bags from my pack and asked him to fill one each with tsampa and sugar. As an afterthought I also bought matches and a candle. If the worst came to the worst, I thought, I could always eat the candle.

I left Dhorpatan with a westerly wind in my face and the sun high in a cloudless sky. The light in this valley seemed to have a crystalline quality to it, an intensity I had not found before but was to notice again and again as I walked west. Its luminescence made the mountains glisten, and I remembered observing this strange characteristic once before in Patagonia. It comes, I believe, not just with altitude but with remoteness from populated areas – a combination of rarefied and absolutely unpolluted air. Many high places are deprived of it by smoke from towns or forest fires or by fumes from traffic, which may be carried on the wind for as much as a thousand miles to filter the sunlight over whole mountain ranges. The northern Rockies suffer badly in this way, as indeed do many parts of the Himalaya when the trade winds blow up from the Ganga plain. I reminded myself that the pure sunlight now illuminating my progress was for much of the world a long forgotten luxury. I drank it in. Skipping down the path, I waved cheerily to a shepherd and his flock away to my right. Both shepherd and sheep were the same dusty beige as the earth across which they moved. As I watched he waved back, then melted into his surroundings like a mirage and the hillside was empty again.

The path descended to the Uttar Ganga and crossed it on a wooden bridge. The bridge was a welcome sight: well used and well maintained. At intervals along it wooden effigies had been put on guard to protect travellers from the *bhuts*, or demons, that many Nepalese still believe lie in wait for travellers at particularly difficult spots. I have to say that they were the ugliest effigies I had ever seen: perfect, I should imagine, for the job. I patted the last on its bald head and started to climb.

Tudken had warned me about the lack of food along the way, but what he hadn't mentioned was that for the next day and a half not a single running stream would cross my path. I climbed for two hours until I was walking 1,000 feet above the river. The path followed a ledge and occasionally dived down to cross a side valley decanting into the gorge below. Each time it did so I strained my ears for the sound of water, and each time the wind in the trees played tricks on me, imitating the trickle of a stream so perfectly that my heart leaped and thumped until I was actually standing on the bank of the stream itself, staring in disbelief at its dried-up bed.

I camped on a tiny platform, the remains of a long-abandoned barley terrace less than four feet wide. Out of sight, the Uttar Ganga raged through its canyon. Perched like an eagle in this eyrie, and suffering probably from the first stages of dehydration, I felt a strange detachment as I looked around. My senses of vertical and horizontal had already been stretched to the limit; now the dimensions seemed to be merging into one, so that I could no longer be sure whether if I stepped off the platform I would plunge into the gorge below, or float away like Mary Poppins with her umbrella. My tent was pegged so close to the edge that if I rolled over in my sleep I might easily find out.

With obsessive care I measured out the last of my remaining water: half for that evening and half for the morning. I put the evening's ration in the saucepan, added some tea and set it on my butane stove just inside the tent. It was almost boiling when the inevitable happened. I turned to pick up the mug, caught the stove with my sleeve and pulled stove, saucepan and boiling water on top of me. For a moment I had a vision of the tent about to be engulfed in flames. I grabbed the stove and managed to extinguish it, ignoring the scalding tea sloshing over me. I sat for a full minute looking balefully at the singed groundsheet and the empty saucepan, then buried my head in my hands.

My sleep was disturbed by a howling wind, a raging thirst, smarting burns and nightmares about Julie Andrews. Next morning I rose late. I was frightened and didn't want to get out of my sleeping bag. I used the last of the water to brew some tea and managed not to spill it this time. Then I opened the tent-flaps and gasped in horror at what I saw. The wind had torn out the guy-ropes where I had pegged them to the overhanging crags. Completely unsupported, the tent had shifted slightly and was now half on the platform and half in space. Only the weight of my body was holding it to the canyon wall. Even Mary Poppins would have winced. I forgot about my thirst and burns and nightmares, and slithered gently, oh so carefully, out of the sleeping bag and back on to the platform, pulling the tent up behind me. I wasted no time in decamping from this dreadful spot, and within ten minutes was on my way.

All morning I looked desperately for signs of water, but the streams were dry just as before. The Uttar Ganga roared mockingly at me from its gorge. But the path was descending

1   Jashara Maya of Phalenksangu – one of many villagers in the Marsyangdi Valley who, since 1977, have opened their houses to trekkers.

2   Approaching Lumsum and the Jaljala Pass. The Dhaulagiri massif blocks the valley ahead, with the summit of Churen Himal (24,150 feet) just visible left of centre.

3   The Khatyar Khola valley after the blizzard. The trail had already been re-established by villagers walking barefoot in the snow.

4   A pilgrim immerses himself on the steps of one of Varanasi's riverside *ghats*: 'oblivious to everything except the Ganga and the rising sun'.

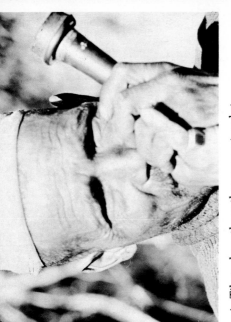

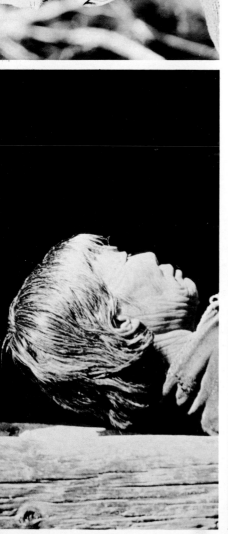

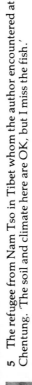

5 The refugee from Nam Tso in Tibet whom the author encountered at Chentung. 'The soil and climate here are OK, but I miss the fish.'

6 Seera's headman, Debi Lal Burathuki, relaxes with his clay *tamakhu*. Marijuana is still freely smoked in the remoter villages – an alternative to alcohol when there is insufficient surplus rice and barley to brew beer or distil spirits.

7 A quarter of a century after the closure of the Tibetan border, ancient trade links still survive. Here, a Tibetan porter heads towards Jumla with a consignment of wool.

8 An *ohar-dohar garne dungaa* ('coming-and-going canoe-boat') picks its way cautiously across the Thuli Bheri.

9 Suspension bridges have replaced dugout canoes on most river crossings. Although undoubtedly more secure, they can still provide a challenge to timid travellers – and an entertaining spectacle for the locals.

10 A fast food joint at Ghorepani on the Annapurna Circuit. Coke, beer, rum, and despair.

11 Jumla bazaar. In the foreground, Chhetri women carrying wicker *dokos* come in from the surrounding hills. Note the kerosene streetlights – until 1983 Jumla's only visible concession to the twentieth century.

12 Reaping the rice harvest west of Pokhara, late November. Women and children use *khukris* to cut the crop.

13 Threshing rice on the shores of Phewa Tal. The animals' trampling separates the grains.

14 The main street of Seera, a Bhotia village on the Uttar Ganga. Log steps lead to the street above.

15 Travelling musicians near Darbang. The brass section could be heard three miles away.

16 The National Kabbadi Championships at Mahendranagar.

17 Porters, goat-herders and the author share a smoke before tackling the climb to Chakhure Lekh.

now, and by midday it was clear that it was going to rejoin the
river. My spirits rose, and as I rounded the final bend I saw
that at the point where it reached the river-bank a village had
been built into the canyon wall. It was completely different
from any of the villages I had been through so far. Its box-like
houses were built almost on top of each other, the roof of one
acting as the verandah of the one above. The streets of the
village were formed by linking each verandah with the next.
Rough-hewn logs provided the vertical connections, their
insides hollowed out to make steps. This was a village of the
Bhotia people who came from Tibet to Nepal several centuries
ago. Their architecture was very different from that of the
more recent immigrants I had met in Dhorpatan. If this was an
example of the sort of site the Bhotias chose for their villages, I
could see why.

I made a beeline for the river and knelt down like a camel
and drank. It took several minutes to quench my thirst. When
I finally straightened up and turned round I found the entire
village standing behind me, watching in astonishment. I don't
suppose they were used to passers-by, and certainly not ones
who made such dramatic entrances. I suddenly realised how
comical I must have looked, and laughed. The village laughed
back. Two of them came forward and motioned me to follow
them. Belching slightly from my indulgence at the river-bank,
I climbed two flights of log steps and was led to a box slightly
larger than the rest, the residence of the *panchayat* leader or
village headman.

The headman sat on his verandah and beamed. His wrinkles belied his youth, and he used them to good effect to create
an aura of dignity and wisdom. I was most impressed by him
and noticed the rest of the village was too. He introduced
himself as Debi Lal Burathuki – an unusual combination of
Hindu and Buddhist names indicating probably mixed
descent – and informed me that the village's name was Seera.
The rest of the inhabitants, who had crowded round to listen,
were shooed away and I sat down with the headman's own
family to explain about my walk. A pipe was passed around,
the stubby clay *tamakhu* so beloved of country people in

Nepal. I found this extraordinarily difficult to use, since it lacked what to me appeared an essential feature, the right-angled bend in the stem. It was kept alight by hot embers, taken from the headman's hearth and balanced on a mound of tobacco in the bowl. Each time my turn came to smoke the tamakhu the embers somehow ended up not in the bowl but burning holes in my trousers.

Debi Lal Burathuki had just had to make a difficult decision. The year's harvest had been a disappointing one – enough to feed only eighty people through the winter, which presented something of a problem because the population of the village was a hundred and twenty. The village had agreed that forty should leave to fend for themselves until the spring, and had looked to the headman to decide which they should be. It was a grave responsibility because some of the forty would undoubtedly not survive. I was horrified by this and said so. The headman shrugged it off as if it happened quite often. 'It is the will of the Buddha,' he said.

One of Debi Lal Burathuki's young sons had a nasty rash on his head, and the headman asked if I could do anything for him. This presented me with something of a dilemma. I am no doctor and would probably not have been able to do much even if I had been. To do a little and raise the family's hopes might cause more harm than doing nothing at all. But the sores were suppurating badly and I couldn't refuse. I bathed them and applied liberal quantities of antiseptic cream, finishing off the treatment with a smart bandage. Everyone seemed to like this, especially the boy. Debi Lal Burathuki disappeared indoors and emerged holding a jar of sticky brown liquid which he pronounced to be *maha* and presented to me with a flourish. I looked at it doubtfully. '*Maha*,' he insisted, '*Maha!*' Getting quite excited now, he rose to his feet and ran the full length of the verandah, waving his arms like wings and going 'Bzzzzz!' until at last I tasted the sticky substance and found to my delight that it was honey: rhododendron honey to be exact, one of the most sought-after delicacies in Nepal. It was my turn to beam. I tried without success to pay something for this magnificent gift. '*Ke bhaau paisaa ho?'* asked the headman with a worldly look on his face: 'What would I do with money?' I couldn't think of a sensible reply.

From Seera the walk became an act of will. The path climbed immediately back to the high ridges, then dived down to the river again. A second time it climbed, then embarked on a series of colossal sweeps as it picked its way across half a dozen side valleys, each larger than almost any valley in Europe. In two days I climbed the equivalent of four Snowdons – with no café at the top. I was walking perhaps five times the distance that the crow would have flown. I knew, because there were a lot of crows flying down the Uttar Ganga and I watched them do it.

To help me up the hills I started talking to myself. 'Come on Pilkington, where are your GUTS?' What was that rubbish about wanting to understand how people coped with hardships in the mountains? Why, you can't even cope with the foothills!'

I tried singing one of those old Bruce Springsteen songs about the endless road. '*Like a river that don't know where it's flowing, I took a wrong turn and I just kept going.* Tiddley pom.'

· The path passed through another Bhotia village where the people shot hostile looks at me from their verandahs. Perhaps they had heard my rendering of 'Johnny B. Goode' floating across the valley. I gave them a few lines of 'Hit me with your Rhythm Stick' and they all ran indoors.

Just beyond this village the Uttar Ganga joined the Sani Bheri, the 'Little Bheri', a foaming torrent which came in from the north. If this was considered little, I shuddered to think what the Great Bheri would be like. The path zigzagged down to a crazy cantilever bridge which sagged beneath my weight to within inches of the rushing water. Then it climbed past yet another Bhotia village and began a long traverse high above the gorge.

I was encountering other wayfarers now, and had to curb the singing, talking, scratching, belching and other unpleasant habits I had fallen into whilst walking alone. It wasn't that I was ashamed of them, but to the people of the Uttar Ganga and Sani Bheri I must have appeared perfectly outrageous anyway; there was no need to dramatise the point. I was sure that if a Bhotia found himself walking down Oxford Street he would resist the temptation to squat outside Selfridge's, relieve himself, then burst into the chorus of a Bhotia travelling song. I felt likewise.

The path dropped back to the river and disappeared in a jumble of boulders, each the size of a double decker bus. I picked my way over them like an ant in a gravel pit. One boulder had a fifteen foot face down which I abseiled on a guy-rope from my tent – not a method I would recommend. No sooner was I through these than I was climbing another Snowdon, and halfway up I was on my knees again. False summit followed false summit; there seemed to be no end.

A Hindu in his late teens had been watching my progress from his house at the top of the hill, and now he came running down and grasped my hand. '*Aaunus, aaunus!*' he insisted. 'Come, it is only a few steps more.' Seeing the watery look in my eyes, he ran indoors to stoke up his fire, then re-emerged and beckoned me inside. At my sudden appearance in the middle of her living room his young wife went into a flat spin; she ran to a corner, buried her face in her shawl and whimpered. I turned to leave but the young man would have none of it. With a gesture worthy of the stage he laid out a rug, then held out both hands. 'Me-a Dabur Bahadur,' he announced proudly. 'We-al-come!'

Dabur Bahadur was very self-assured for one so young. He seemed keen to show me his worldliness – and also his English which, he said, he had learned at secondary school. At first the conversation followed the usual course: where was I going, where had I come from, the price of my boots. Then to my dismay he grasped my feet. 'You give-a boots Dabur Bahadur!'

I'm ashamed to say that the rest of the evening passed in animated discussion as to why, when I was obviously so rich, I couldn't make a gift to poor Dabur Bahadur of my measly pair of boots. I pointed to the distance I still had to walk; Dabur Bahadur said he walked that far every month. I pleaded that I had only just broken them in; he said that if I walked barefoot I wouldn't have to worry about such irritations. I even tried to persuade him that they belonged to my Granny, but that didn't wash either. I was too exhausted to put up a spirited defence and too exhausted to leave. Finally I said in the best Nepali I could muster, 'Dabur Bahadur, you are a rogue and a scoundrel and a disgrace to the name Bahadur!' This was really a bit unfair because, as you may have noticed, almost everybody in Nepal is called Bahadur. Nevertheless it worked; Dabur Bahadur blushed deeply, looked at his feet for a few minutes, then said coyly, 'Do you know the Beatles?'

I left next morning complete with boots (I had hidden them inside my sleeping bag). After a few miles the valley widened considerably and the river became twisting and braided on a broad floodplain. I stopped for lunch on a grassy promontory and took in the details of this new scene. The floodplain was intensively farmed, and from my vantage point I could make out dozens of figures at work. Some fields were being ploughed, using oxen or water buffalo to draw the wooden ploughshares through the soil. Others were already being planted with winter wheat or barley. It was a relief after the desolation of the Uttar Ganga to see such signs of civilisation again, but I was hardly prepared for what happened next. Round the corner came a man with – of all things – a transistor radio. He sat down beside me and turned it up.

'*Namaste sahib!*'

'Hello.'

'*Tapaaiko desh America ho?* – Are you from America?'

'Well, no actually, I'm from England.'

'*Thik chha* – that's nice.' A pause. 'I've heard lots of stories about America.'

'But I'm not from America.'

'No, no. Of course not.'

Pause.

'Are people in America very rich?'

85

'Well, I'm afraid I wouldn't know, because I'm not American.'

'Ah yes. I remember you said.'

Pause.

'Which part of America is England in?'

The radio was chattering inanely to itself. I told him to please switch it off or go away because it was spoiling my lunch. He smiled sweetly and switched it to another channel. 'PISS OFF!' I yelled. He seemed to understand this. He scuttled away muttering, to be replaced almost immediately by an old gent who coughed yellow sputum all over my tsampa. It was no more than I deserved.

At the village of Jipu I found to my surprise that there was an inn, run by a most hospitable innkeeper with the help of his family which, as far as I could make out, comprised half the population of Jipu. In Nepal 'family' has a much wider meaning than the small and well-defined group of husband, wife, parents and children which we would regard as making up a family in the West. The Nepali language gives a clue to its extent by its vocabulary for different forms of kinship – some fifty words in all. The immediate family is taken to include every member of a particular generation, so that children may be found calling their aunts 'mother', their uncles 'father' and their cousins 'sisters and brothers'. A few of the terms are also used by unrelated people as polite forms of address. Thus any woman may be called *didi* ('sister') and an old man, as a mark of special affection or respect, may be referred to as *baabu* or 'father'.

The innkeeper's name was Hark. As it was nearly Christmas I sang him a verse of 'Hark, the Herald Angels Sing'. My evening meal of lentils and bread was prepared by a woman whom he introduced as his sister, but might of course have been a cousin or girlfriend. Whoever she was, by the morning she was gone. Hark himself produced breakfast, which he served to me in bed, a much appreciated luxury, watched by the remainder of Jipu through the open door. I'm afraid Hark will never make a businessman; after I had paid him a paltry sum for my board and lodging he decided he had overcharged me and made me take half of it back.

Shortly after Jipu the Sani Bheri turned south towards Jajarkot and Surkhet, and I turned north towards the Thuli or Great Bheri. An 8,000 foot pass separated the two rivers here. Reluctantly I started climbing again. A small boy called Gom accompanied me for much of the day, telling me the Nepalese names of the things along the way and repeating them until I got the pronunciation just right. Gom shared sweet bananas with me from his tattered shoulder bag, and I was glad to be able to share some biscuits in return, a treat for both of us. Then at midday we arrived at the first shop I had come across in more than a week. It was perched in a cleft between two valleys, at a strategic point where several paths met. Rummaging through its dusty shelves I found a mirror, and was horrified to see that my face was almost black. I rubbed it to see if it was dirt or suntan; it was dirt. I grimaced and set the whole shop sniggering.

Gom pointed out my route to the pass – a hot and thirsty four-hour climb. I stopped to drink from a stream that ran alongside the path. 'No, not from there!' insisted a passing woman. '*Tyo paani naraamro chha* – that water's not good. Drink from the *khola*, the river further along the way.' Until this moment I had suspected the Nepalese of having little discrimination in their use of water for drinking, for washing and for the other necessities of life. I had sterilised almost everything I drank. Now I realised that even in the countryside a careful distinction was maintained; you just had to know which was which. As a traveller I would obviously be liable to make mistakes, so I still sterilised everything when I could. But from now on I started asking people if the water was *raamro* or *naraamro* – good or bad – and always got an unequivocal reply.

I crossed the pass as the sun went down, and by the time I had found a place flat enough to camp it was completely dark. I was groping with my tent when three Hindus came up; they had heard the dreadful din I was making with my aluminium poles. It seemed odd that three Hindus should be here in the

87

middle of nowhere after dark, but no odder than many of the other things that had happened in the last few weeks. They watched quietly as I banged the tent-pegs in.

It was while I was doing this that a feeling came over me that all was not quite as it should be. I may get a bit scatter-brained after a hard day, but even so I felt that the hummocky grass on which I was pitching my tent shouldn't really have lights and voices coming from underneath it. Very slowly I realised the awful truth. These men who were watching me so politely lived here. I had just set up camp on their roof.

It is an endearing and edifying characteristic of the Nepalese that however sorely you may try their patience you hardly ever see them rattled. Sometimes their magnanimity seems to approach saintliness. Time and again I blundered into people's lives to be greeted simply with a broad smile and a dismissive wave towards the trampled crop or the panicking buffalo or goat. This time, however, I was sure I had gone too far. What should I say? What *could* I say? I tried to imagine what I would say if someone tried to pitch a tent on my roof. It was unimaginable (it has a thirty-degree slope). Finally I just stammered my apologies and waited. The Hindus slowly and deliberately examined the half-erected tent – pride of my belongings and of Blacks of Greenock – then turned pityingly to me. One of them spoke. 'That doesn't look very comfort-able. Would you like to come and sleep in our house?'

There followed an evening of banter and mimicry, of ribbing and leg-pulling, such as you can only have with someone who has just tried to camp on your roof. I left the tent and followed my impromptu hosts downstairs to where some women were roasting roti round a glowing hearth. My company seemed to have been anticipated; there was far too much food for us all. As we feasted, they complimented me on my Nepali and at the same time apologised that there wasn't more to eat – observations which were both equally absurd.

I slept in an outhouse, and as the laughter from the house died away I became aware of another sound. From far away across the Thuli Bheri drums were beating a syncopated

rhythm through the night. I lay back and listened, wondering
drowsily what they signified. My hosts had warned me that in
crossing the Bheri I would be entering a region of new people,
new customs and new problems. For one thing I would no
longer be in a land of plenty. Between the Bheri and the Seti
the harvest had failed for two years running; from now on, the
question would be not what food was available, but whether
there was any food at all.

The next morning, however, was one of those when everything seems to fall into place. For once the trail was unmistakable and went straight down the valley, following the river
instead of winding up and down all the tributary valleys to
visit every village on the mountainside. The sun shone out of a
clear blue sky, and I reached the Thuli Bheri, my day's
objective, by mid-morning.

I had been told that food and a bridge would be available
here. Food there certainly was, in the shape of bananas which
a woman was selling at twenty paisaa – a little under 1p –
each, but the bridge was still under construction and by all
appearances had a long way to go. Instead the woman waved
me towards *ohar-dohar garne dungaa*, 'the coming-and-going
canoe-boat'.

Before the advent of steel suspension bridges in Nepal, the
larger rivers used to be crossed by primitive ferries, paddled by
bony old ferrymen who knew every eddy and eccentricity of
the turbulent currents. They often capsised; indeed, their safety
record was so bad that some said it was a wonder there were
any bony old ferrymen left. This one was no exception. The
craft was a hollowed-out tree trunk which, being rudderless,
was guided by the old-timer with his paddle. As he helped me
aboard it sank to the gunwales. There were already several
pools of water in the bottom. Gesturing me to squat down in
one of them and stay still, the ferryman slipped the painter and
pushed off into the current. Within seconds we catapulted a
hundred yards downstream, entered a whirlpool, revolved
several times and then without warning were propelled violently broadside, as if by an unseen hand, towards the far

shore. I exhaled softly as we left the main current and drifted in. The ferryman grasped the bank and smiled. 'That will be twenty-five paisaa, sahib,' he croaked in a matter of fact fashion.

Surviving this watery episode in the walk greatly heartened me. Since I was walking from east to west – across the grain of a country where most of the drainage is from north to south – I had already crossed several substantial rivers and knew I would have to cross several more. With the experience of the Thuli Bheri ferry under my belt I now felt ready to tackle the ones that lay ahead. Full of verve, I pressed on to the village of Dalli where the Thuli Bheri was joined by the Sama Khola – the river I was to follow up to the passes that led to Jumla. On the bank of this surging tributary, just where it emerged from a cleft to join the main river, I found to my delight a group of inns. Sadly my expectations were premature; all they seemed able to muster between them was buffalo milk and some rather mouldy bread. I didn't dally in Dalli. An hour later I was asleep under the stars, with a new moon chasing the sun down to the western horizon. A cold breeze blew; I snuggled deep inside my sleeping bag, tired, supperless, but confident. How often pride comes before a fall!

There are basically two ways to reach Jumla from the southeast. One crosses Chakhure Lekh, reaching 13,000 feet before dropping down to the Tila Khola and turning west to Jumla. The other rises to 15,000 feet on Thakurji Lekh and approaches Jumla from the south. Both are difficult routes and in December their high sections would be covered with snow. I had decided to wait and see what local people thought of them before making up my mind which one to take.

As it turned out, I had no time anyway to worry about my choice of routes because I spent most of the next day struggling to reach the point where they forked. The map, as usual, was no help. It showed a major trail going straight up the valley on an impossibly direct course; obviously someone had nudged the cartographer at a critical moment. Casting about for clues, I came upon an old man of the road who convinced me that the best way was to follow the right bank of the river. I went in the direction he pointed.

The path was clear enough for the first mile or so, then became fainter as the valley closed in. Soon it was just a rocky ledge sandwiched between the river and the vertical sides of an ever-narrowing canyon. The going got steadily more difficult as the canyon became little more than a defile, a cleft in the landscape hundreds of feet deep – I didn't know how many, I couldn't see the top. Beneath me the river crashed and thumped, so completely filling the chasm with sound that I couldn't even comfort myself with my awful singing. After half an hour of this I came to a hideous bit where the slabs of rock forming the ledge sloped steeply towards the water. They were drenched by a waterfall from somewhere above and were green with slime. I inched my way forward, hoping my boots would hold. I scoured the rock for fingerholds but there were none. My pack kept threatening to topple me into the river but it was too late to think about taking it off. Each unnecessary movement would be an invitation to almost certain death. A fist-sized boulder detached itself from the rocks above, whistled past my nose and disintegrated at my feet. I panicked, half turned to go back, then changed my mind. That would be madness. But to go forward seemed madness too. I hung on by my fingertips and concentrated on pizza.

All of a sudden I was through. The ledge widened and I scrambled on to a patch of tufty grass, lying there for several minutes until a second boulder hurtling down from above spurred me into action again. I progressed another hundred yards without difficulty – then saw to my horror that the path disappeared straight into the river, to emerge a little way upstream on the opposite bank.

I stared at the white water for a long time. It looked very cold and not at all inviting, but I certainly wasn't going to brave the ledge again, so after putting off the moment as long as possible I took a big stick and a deep breath, and waded in. The stick was a technique I had learned in Bolivia in the rainy season. You face the current, plant it on the river-bed upstream, put all your weight on it, move one foot, then the other, then move the stick and start all over again. It is an agonisingly slow way of crossing a river, but on several occasions it has saved me from being swept away. This time I was lucky; the water only came up to my thighs. I was quickly across and making progress again. Soon I could see where the proper trail had gone up the mountainside to avoid the canyon. It rejoined my own route a mile or so upstream. I smiled grimly to myself; the old man of the road had saved me a few hundred feet of climbing, but in doing so had nearly sent me to my death.

Local opinion was firmly in favour of the Chakhure Lekh route, so I plumped for that. It was a wide path, pounded out over the centuries by the hooves of yak caravans carrying flour and rice to the remote northern districts of Mugu and Humla, and returning with salt and wool from Tibet. At the point where it began the climb out of the valley, a group of men stood outside a small inn, with a herd of goats in an enclosure beyond. They had just brought the animals over from Jumla, and assured me that the route was passable as the winter snows had not yet arrived. Muttering that I trusted they wouldn't come while I was there, I looked hopefully towards the inn for something to eat.

In the valleys west of the Thuli Bheri houses are usually of two storeys, the lower one for animals and the upper one for the family. Often the upstairs consists simply of one great room, with an open hearth in the middle. Sometimes there is a separate inner room for sleeping. And very occasionally there is a verandah for accommodating people like me. The houses have mud walls and beautifully carved wooden windows and doors. The outsides are either whitewashed or painted ochre, and are frequently decorated by children with pictures of flowers, trees and birds. Access to the human accommodation is gained by mud steps leading to a tiny Alice-in-Wonderland doorway, sometimes no more than three feet high. It was through this door that I was led, or rather squeezed, into the inn by its jolly owner and plied with beans and chapatis till I was quite sure I wouldn't be able to squeeze out again.

The approach to the pass was a two-day walk through pine forests and high grassy pastures. The pastures were used for summer grazing, but now, in December, they were deserted and serene. I would like to be able to say that I was totally alone in this wilderness, but as I was leaving the inn one of the goat herders thrust a small man in my direction, gave me a wry grin and said, 'Here's someone to keep you company.' The victim was a grizzled old porter, on his way to Jumla with a load of cooking oil, with legs so spindly that when he took up his cargo it seemed as if he would collapse in a heap of skin and bones. He was the only person I met on the whole of my walk who actually went more slowly than I did. Time and again I thought I had shaken him off, only to look back and see his diminutive figure struggling towards me. I made camp early in a meadow by a stream, and was just turning in when he arrived in pitch darkness. He looked all in. We had a cup of tea together, but he declined my offer to share my tent, perhaps thinking (quite rightly) that I would be too smelly at such close quarters. Hunched in a blanket, he sat all night stoking a pathetic camp fire, whose faint glow greeted me each time I poked my head out of the tent.

Diary, 20 December 1982

I wonder what he's thinking over there, as he stares forlornly into the fire? He doesn't speak a word of any language I have ever come across, so I am unlikely to find out. In a whole day I haven't even so much as discovered his name. Until I do, I have decided to call him Percy porter.

It's good to have even Percy porter's melancholy company in this bleak place. Shortly after the sun went down the wolves started howling, and just five minutes ago I heard the blood-curdling laughing call of a hyena. The tent seems such flimsy protection against these hideous creatures. My only weapon is the six-inch knife from my cutlery canteen, and for what it's worth I'll sleep with it by my side. But I'm aware of how easily a single mishap could turn this adventure into a nightmare. I doubt somehow whether Percy porter would respond very well in an emergency. I've got to face the fact that if I need help now, the only person who is going to provide it is me. I hope my resourcefulness will not be stretched too far.

December the twenty-first, the winter solstice, was perhaps not the most sensible day to choose to cross a 13,000 foot pass that would involve ten hours' hard walking. I struck camp in the freezing cold before dawn, and was going for more than an hour before the sun struggled over the horizon to thaw my numbed fingers and toes. Percy porter was up and off earlier still, but I soon caught him up, and we played cat and mouse all morning. As the sun caught each meadow it seemed to spring to life. Ice melted into rivulets; choughs and snow pigeons fluttered their wings; mouse hares darted from burrow to burrow, and a troupe of langur monkeys crossed my path, aware of my presence but quite unconcerned. The Himalayan langur, unlike its leaf-eating cousin of the plains, often comes down from the trees and ranges across open hillsides, preferring the more tasty diet of herbs and berries that can be reached from the ground. It has been observed up to 14,000 feet: the highest-altitude primate in the world. The langurs of Nepal weigh three stone or more – which is a lot as monkeys go – but I had been assured that they were not given to throwing it around; in fact they are well known for their passive disposition. Whether this cordiality is due to their mountain habitat or their vegetarian diet has never been clarified, but the reputation seems well deserved. The worst case of aggression I heard of was when a troupe took exception to a trekker who had blundered through some trees where they were sleeping. They huddled on their bough, waited till he was directly underneath, then pissed on him.

I sat down where the path began its 5,000 foot climb to the pass, and waited for Percy porter. He arrived as usual in a state of collapse. We shared some biscuits and I said I wanted to get going straight away, to be over the top by dusk. He claimed this was impossible, and looking at him I could believe it. He said he would stay the night where he was, but assured me that if I wanted to go on, I would find the path quite easily, with water along the way. An hour later, looking back, I was surprised to see his hunched form following me again at a snail's pace far below. But his spurt of energy must have been short-lived, because that glimpse was the last I ever saw of Percy porter.

It was a loathsome climb. The summit retreated steadily (as you may have noticed many summits do). After four hours my legs were on the point of giving up. I was walking so slowly that a lizard ran across my boot, unaware that the boot was attached to a moving body. In spite of Percy porter's assurances there was no water from the point where I left him until the foot of the pass on the far side, where I arrived in darkness, many hours later, after a running descent. With a neat sense of irony the place was called Napaani – 'no water'. Percy porter was doomed to spend a night with no water, no firewood and just a thin blanket to keep him warm. He had been a porter all his life and had no doubt survived worse. But I shuddered at the thought, gave silent thanks for my better luck, and pressed on through the night to the first village on the other side.

I arrived very late and made for the only house with lights showing. Sounds of merrymaking came from within. I didn't knock; the door was wide open and I could see that no one would have heard me if I had.

To get an idea of the scene inside, you really need to have been in the 'Frog and Frigate' by Southampton docks at closing time on a Saturday night. A log fire blazed in the hearth and a dozen men were sitting or standing round it, smoking hand-rolled cigarettes and drinking from bowls of what I took to be chang. Three of them had *saarangis* – small stringed instruments like primitive fiddles – and were playing them for all they were worth. The others were belting out the words to what sounded like a Nepalese version of 'Knees up Mother Brown'. They were oblivious to my presence. I put down my pack by the door and tried to make out the words of the song. As with most pub songs, it was impossible. At length one of the men staggered over, drew me into the circle and thrust a bowl of chang into my hand. He had wild hair, a pirate's moustache and big gold earrings – just like the landlord at the 'Frog and Frigate'. Another man gave me a bagful of wild walnuts and I almost expected to see GOLDEN WONDER printed on it. I felt immediately at home.

As the evening wore on it became apparent that everyone was expected to make a contribution to the entertainment in some way or other. One man told a story; another danced a jig; a boy who looked too young to be drinking gave a moving rendition of a shepherd's song in a voice that was almost operatic. I decided to give them 'The Lion and Albert'. I'm not sure if the subtler nuances of Stanley Holloway's cameo of Lancashire life were fully understood in this village under the shadow of Chakhure Lekh. Nevertheless, it won me a round of applause, slaps on the back and a considerable further quantity of chang. Fickle Yorkshireman that I am.

Had I been in any state to think about it, I might have dwelt that evening on the fact that I had now passed from the Bheri and its tributaries into the basin of the Karnali which drains most of Nepal's north-west. The Karnali region was said to be more rugged, arid and generally inhospitable than any I had passed through so far, and from the top of the pass I had seen that this description was fully accurate. Jagged peaks had formed a serrated, snow-capped horizon on three points of the compass. Nearby to the east Bhalu Lekh had been a mass of shattered granite; to the north the Kanjirobas, a range rising to 23,000 feet which escaped the foot of man until as recently as 1973, had presented the appearance of a wall of rock and ice; and to the north-west and west the lekhs had rolled on, one behind another, to the pinnacle of Api where India, China and Nepal came together more than a hundred miles away. These wonders now lay silently under the stars, waiting to be discovered and explored. I lay silently under the table where I had gracefully slid, eyes closed, a perky smile on my face, my chang bowl still cradled in my arms.

The valley I was now in was that of the Tila Khola which flows north-west to Jumla, then south-west to join the Karnali some sixty miles downstream. I opened my eyes and watched the sun melting icicles outside the open window. According to my diary this morning was 22 December. It looked as if I would be in Jumla in time for Christmas.

Jumla was to be quite a significant point on my walk. The largest settlement in the whole of Nepal's western mountains, it was a place where I hoped to be able to replenish my food supplies, do some washing, repair my clothes, and above all for a few days shirk the daily routine of striking camp and walking which had by now lost some of its novelty. It was not yet a month since I had left Pokhara, but I felt that I needed a break.

The temperature was still well below freezing when I left the scene of the previous night's revelry. Nobody stirred. The path followed the river into a gorge where the sun had not yet penetrated, and frost carpeted the ground. Where streams crossed I found that the trickling water had frozen layer upon layer like the icing on a Christmas cake. The path plunged beneath these icy blankets, to reappear tantalisingly a dozen yards further on. I learned to scramble over these impossibly slippery obstacles ignominiously on all fours. Once I went skating off downstream, to land with a splash and a squawk where the stream became liquid again. Other travellers chuckled mercilessly at these antics. It was most unfair: they seemed to be able to walk over the ice as if it wasn't there.

Everyone agreed that Jumla was now no more than a day's walk away, but it took two hard and uncomfortable days before I saw the cluster of prayer flags and neat whitewashed houses where the Chaudhabise Khola joined the Tila. Several paths converged to cross the two rivers and the last mile to the bazaar was thronged with travellers from the surrounding hills. It was market day. The path rang out with the shouts of friends being recognised and the chatter of news being exchanged, and I strained my ears to understand the new dialects. Walnuts, apples and apricots were passed around in a wave of excitement which mounted as we covered the last few hundred yards like a wave approaching a beach. I was swept along in the mêlée. A small cheer went up as we marched through late afternoon shadows into Jumla's single cobbled street.

6

Jumla to RaRa Tal

'For me there is only the travelling on paths
that have heart, on any path that may have
heart. There I travel, and the only worth-
while challenge is to traverse its full length.
And there I travel, looking, looking, breath-
lessly.'

Carlos Castaneda,
The Teachings of Don Juan

Coming into Jumla after three weeks in the mountains, I
found in its impoverished mud and wood buildings an aura of
sophistication and excitement quite out of proportion to their
miserable collapsing frontages. I gaped at the shops like a
tourist on a package holiday. What luxuries lurked behind
those rickety counters! I felt I had landed in a place flowing
with milk and honey, and on closer inspection found this to
be perfectly true. There was yak milk from the dairy on the
Guthichaur road; rhododendron honey from the Chinese
general store by the stream which burbled its way through the
stony fields behind the bazaar.

The vast scale of Jumla's setting – a broad valley flanked by
forested slopes rising seemingly to the sky – belittled the town
and belied its own elevation of more than 7,500 feet. But
evidence that this was a high-altitude community was all
around me, and once I had got over my initial awe I opened
my eyes and began to see. The people busying themselves in
the bazaar were small and wiry, with the same broad chests
that I had first seen among the Quechua Indians of the
Peruvian *altiplano*. I noticed how the black soil had worked
its way into their clothes and skin, making them appear

several shades darker than the people from the lowlands – an effect no doubt aided by years of sitting around smoky juniper fires. They haggled in Jumli, a language dating from the eleventh century, which bears little resemblance to either Tibetan or modern Nepali. Jumli has become a symbol by which Jumla's 5,000 citizens express their steely independence from Kathmandu. People would buttonhole me in conversation with the linguistic fervour of a Basque or a Welshman, which was rather awkward because I didn't understand a single word they said.

To extract a living from the thin upland soil, earlier inhabitants created one of the most intricate irrigation systems in the whole of the Himalaya, with channels several feet wide running back and forth across the hillsides to water every nook of cultivable land. Using this legacy, Jumla's present residents were returning good harvests of the by now familiar wheat, barley, potatoes and millet, with occasional crops of mustard seed and soya beans. But in addition, many fields were given over to a plant I had never expected to see at such an altitude – rice.

It was not exactly the sort of rice you'd expect to find in a curry house in Wimbledon. The grains were big, red and crunchy, with a rich nutty flavour. I thought I saw terraces going up to more than 9,000 feet; if I was not mistaken, this would be a record matched only by the high-altitude paddy-fields around the Vale of Kashmir. I was not surprised, therefore, to hear that Jumla's own tasty grains came originally from Kashmir. Indeed, it was said that they were brought by the legendary *yogi* Chandannath more than five centuries ago.

Chandannath prescribed a precise and elaborate timetable to nurture the precious crop. On the eleventh day of the Nepalese month of Chait (late March in our calendar), seed beds would be flooded and the seeds soaked for four days. The seeds would then be taken indoors and kept by the fire to encourage sprouting. On the twentieth day of Chait (early April), they would be cast in the paddy-fields, and transplanted during Jeth (late May or early June). Harvesting would take place from Kaartik (October) onwards, depending on the altitude and aspect of the field. Ploughing had to be fitted in before or after the winter snows, and was usually completed only just in time for the next planting season in Chait of the following year. Jumla farmers still adhere strictly to Chandannath's word. In this fourth week of December – the Nepalese month of Pus – I found them ploughing; cajoling their oxen to draw the oaken ploughshares through the paddy-fields before the arrival of the snows.

By a temple in the town centre I came across a lichen-covered stone inscribed 'SRI HANUMAN DHOKA DEKHI KOS 169' – indicating that the Hanuman Dhoka (the old royal palace in Kathmandu) was a distance of 169 *kos* (about 350 miles). This was the first evidence I had seen that the east–west route I was following had any real historical significance. All the trade routes I had encountered so far had been from north to south; indeed, many parts of my own path would have been too narrow for pack animals. The story went that many years ago Jumla rice used to be shipped over the mountains to enrich the palace banquets of the Rana prime ministers, but I had always assumed it had been taken by way of the plains. Here in this weathered stone was evidence that, on the contrary, the small but precious consignments had probably been dispatched along the very same way that I had come.

Jumla in fact lies at a crossing of highways. From the north come several trade routes from the border districts of Mugu and Humla and, until recently, from Tibet. At least one of these has been important since the twelfth century, when the kings of the Malla dynasty used it to reach their summer capital at Sinja. To the south, a wide path winds through valleys and over rolling lekhs to the lowland town of Surkhet; this seven-day journey is the way by which Jumla gets its few imported goods today. To the east, a trail leads to Tarakot and the empty 'snow leopard' domain of Dolpo. And last but not least, on the bluff above Jumla, is the terminal point of a different kind of route: a grassy meadow proudly calling itself Jumla Airport. Services have recently been increased to four light planes per week – yaks on the runway permitting.

At the bottom of my pack I had an introduction to two of the very few Jumla people who weren't Nepalese. Larry and Phyl Asher had left their native Kansas ten years previously to work for the United Mission to Nepal – the organisation which had so patiently tried to teach me Nepali in Kathmandu. In 1980, the UMN had agreed to help the government set up a centre for basic technical education in west Nepal. Everyone had heard of Karnali Technical School, even though it wasn't actually built yet. Larry had been appointed headmaster, and spent hours each day supervising its construction as well as performing more usual headmasterly duties. Phyl had an equally daunting job, instructing students at Jumla's tiny hospital.

Larry, Phyl and their three children were gently preparing for the sort of Christmas you have in Jumla (that is, a quiet one) when I followed the directions given by a dozen sooty hands towards their house. I'm afraid I rather shattered their plans. I must have presented a ghastly appearance as I limped up the muddy lane, because Phyl promptly took me in, plied me with coffee, and without even bothering to ask if I was hungry began to prepare a huge meal. People from the college, the hospital and the town drifted in and out of the small kitchen-cum-living-room, bringing presents of rice or vegetables or asking Phyl's advice on some medical problem. As this went on around us Larry, who had explored most of west

Nepal during his three years in Jumla, proceeded in his lazy midwestern drawl to terrify me about the way ahead. I had explained briefly my plan to walk north to RaRa Tal, then west for 150 miles to India. Larry said encouragingly that clear weather was forecast for the next few days, and this should be long enough for me to reach the lake. My spirits rose. 'After that ... ' his voice trailed off, as if he had been about to say something but had thought better of it.

'After that ... what?' I prompted.

'Oh, probably nothing,' he murmured. 'It's just that the winter storms are due any time now. You might have to stay there till spring.'

The next day, Christmas Eve, while Larry, Phyl and the children opened cards from their family and friends, I pottered round Jumla preparing dutifully but not very enthusiastically for the journey ahead. First on my visiting list was Jagadish Khadka, the Zonal Commissioner for Karnali, whose permission I would need to go to RaRa Tal. I found him behind the Zonal Headquarters with his girlfriend. Yes, he said, of course I could go to RaRa Tal; no, I didn't need his permission in writing; he hoped I would have a nice time and wished me luck. His girlfriend glared at me. It looked as if I had interrupted some important zonal business. I gave them an innocent smile, and, for good measure, a shiny British penny as a memento of the occasion, and bowed out.

Like me, my poor rucksack had also been showing signs of exhaustion, so I nosed around the bazaar for someone who was handy at sewing leather. I found him in a backroom workshop: a wizened old-timer with skin like the material of his profession. His workshop was lined with saddles, bridles and some items of tack that I didn't recognise. It took him twenty minutes to understand what I wanted and five minutes to sew up the fraying parts, a job for which he asked a mere three rupees.

My pack was now ready for the wear and tear ahead, my supplies were replenished from the bazaar and I had been fattened up like a Christmas turkey. It was agreed that I should leave early on Christmas morning, to get over the first of the two passes which barred the way to RaRa Tal that same day. We spent the evening of Christmas Eve sitting round the Ashers' dinner table. After supper had been cleared away the conversation inevitably turned to tales from the mountains. Everybody had their own favourite horror story. Some were about ghosts, some were about demons and some were about travellers disappearing without trace, perhaps carried off by a bear or leopard, or even by the elusive yeti. Other unfortunate wayfarers appeared to have been attacked by bandits, their skulls left by the side of the path as a macabre warning to future passers-by. As at Jashara Maya's in Phalenksangu, I comforted myself with the reminder that stories get hopelessly exaggerated as they pass from mouth to mouth. I knew that I would be most unlikely to meet a bear or a bandit, even less a yeti. But my sleep that night was interspersed with dreams about fierce furry animals, and I was glad when morning came.

I left the Ashers with a heavy pack and a heavier heart. They were the kindest of people and in just two days we had become close friends. Larry walked with me for the first few hundred yards, and after he had said a last goodbye and turned home I stood for several minutes watching him go back down the path. I wanted to return with him, to stay longer with this considerate couple in this curious town. The walk had brought me here but now it was dragging me on. Perhaps in Jumla I had been pampered too much for my own good. Maybe Larry and Phyl had been just a little too hospitable, reminding me of home comforts like coffee and hot showers, and reawakening the part of me that likes a life of luxury. Perhaps, too, an anticlimax was inevitable now. Jumla had been my first goal; the surprising thing was not that I should be reluctant to leave it, but that I had reached it at all. Now, with RaRa Tal so close and the winter snows so imminent, I had no choice but to press on. I turned my back on the town and set out northwards.

I was over the first pass and well into the valley of the Sinja

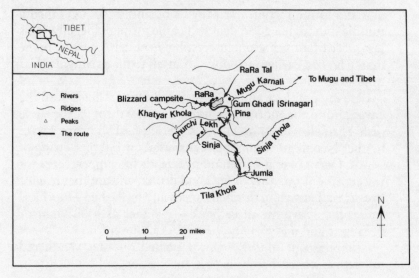

TIBET
NEPAL
INDIA

~~~ Rivers
⌒ Ridges
△ Peaks
← The route

RaRa Tal
Mugu Karnali
To Mugu and Tibet
RaRa
Blizzard campsite
Gum Ghadi (Srinagar)
Khatyar Khola
Pina
Churchi Lekh
Sinja Khola
Sinja
Jumla
Tila Khola

N

0   10   20 miles

5   Jumla to RaRa Tal

Khola when fellow travellers led me away from the path, down to the river and up the face of a cliff to a tea-house in a cave. Its ceiling was blackened with soot, as was its owner. He sent me down the cliff face to bring water in a great brass urn, then cooked potatoes and red rice over a ring of stones. As we warmed ourselves round the cooking pot, the others told me about the village of Mugu where they were heading, fifty miles to the north-east. It sounded like a trading post that had seen better days. From 1843 until 1960 the merchants of Mugu had enjoyed a thriving monopoly on trade between Tibet and west Nepal. They had nurtured it well, moving their village twice before they found a location which was neither too cold for the Khasa traders from the south nor too warm for their Tibetan clientèle from the north. Regular consignments of barley, rice, buckwheat and bamboo changed hands in return for salt, wool, sheep and goats. As recently as the 1950s, my informants said, 1½ million maanaa of salt alone had passed through Mugu by yak or porter every year. I estimated this conservatively to be about 700 tons. Now the border was

105

closed and the fortunes of Mugu's businessmen had taken a tumble – though a good deal still came through illegally. This last piece of information, interestingly enough, came from the man who had earlier introduced himself to me as Mugu's chief of police.

I ate my potatoes and rice hungrily, slept at the back of the cave, and in the morning worked my way through the same dish again for breakfast. The proprietor of the cave spoke neither Nepali nor Jumli, but calculated my bill on a string of beads. I went over it with him: five beads for supper, three for the enormous quantity of tea I had drunk, and another five for breakfast. I gave him thirteen rupees and he flashed a toothless smile, then gave me three back – whether as a discount or because I had misread his abacus I shall never know.

Climbing out of the valley I passed another weathered milestone whose barely legible inscription indicated that it was now 176 kos to Kathmandu. This cheered me up greatly because it meant that since Jumla I had covered no fewer than seven kos. A kos, I should explain, is the distance a Nepalese porter is willing to walk between smokes of his clay pipe or *chilim*. In practice it is a more precise form of measurement than it sounds, because porters are addicted to their pipes and know exactly when their distance is up. It is not very far: about two miles on level ground. But to have covered seven pipe-smokes in rough country in twenty-four hours did seem a solid achievement, and I continued with fresh determination to put a few more under my belt before dusk.

It was this determination which a few hours later got me totally, immovably stuck in a rhododendron thicket. I suppose you could call it the principle of kos and effect. Approaching the second of the two passes I had to cross to reach RaRa, the path divided – the right fork taking a gentler but more circuitous route via the village of Pina, the left fork following the crest of the lekh directly to the lake. At least that was what I had been led to believe. One or two people had added off-handedly that the direct route was not much used, since travellers were usually going to or from Mugu or Tibet, and had no reason to make a detour to the lake. I chose the direct route.

The path started out clearly enough, heading straight up a grassy valley between two pinnacles of rock. The meadows were the home of hundreds of mouse hares – hamster-like creatures which sat basking in the afternoon sunshine until my approaching shadow made them dart back into their burrows. Here and there the soil had been split open as if by a mechanical digger, and I knew from Alaska that this meant I was now in bear country. The Himalayan black bear feeds on these tiny animals, just as the Alaskan grizzly feeds on the gopher. The black bear rarely attacks human beings unless surprised, but all the same I looked round nervously, scanning the hillside for unusual movements. A rustle in the rhododendrons made me start, but turned out to be a Himalayan weasel, disturbed by my approach and curious to know what sort of creature I was. It occurred to me that I had no need to fear catching anything by surprise, because the way had become so overgrown that I was crashing through the scrub like an elephant.

Slowly the path gave up the ghost. Far above I could see where it was supposed to go, but the scrub had become thicker and the snow deeper. I was almost at a standstill. Entangled in the vegetation, I had to crawl on hands and knees to make any progress at all. With a great effort I stood up, parted two frozen rhododendron branches and found myself looking down into a 500 foot ravine lying directly across my path. It was choked with scrub. I decided without a moment's hesitation to call it a day.

The other route, though a lot longer, had the benefit of one of the area's few hotels conveniently placed halfway along it. The Hotel Pina had been highly spoken of all the way from Jumla, so I made for it without ado. Peering into the dimly lit building, I could see the proprietor and his wife huddled round a pitiable log fire. Yes, they said, I would be welcome to stay: I would find their terms very reasonable. They apologised, however, that there was no food available – they had run out of everything except salt and pepper.

As the evening drew on, my hosts in this hotel began to behave in a most extraordinary manner. Hunched over the miserable fire, they tried to cook rice and lentils, looking

107

furtively over their shoulders to see if I had noticed. They whispered to each other conspiratorially in Jumli. Again, furtive glances. Gradually it dawned on me that far from being the proprietors of the Hotel Pina, this clandestine couple were squatters – and so, for that matter, was I. The Hotel Pina had long ago closed its doors, or would have done if it had had any. Business probably hadn't picked up since the Chinese closed the border with Tibet, almost a quarter of a century ago.

RaRa Tal, the largest lake in Nepal, seemed to defy several laws of geography at once. To find a body of water several miles in circumference perched almost a mile up the side of the Mugu Karnali valley would in itself have been remarkable enough. To walk round its eastern end and notice that it was retained by a lip of ground only a few feet above the water level would have been worth noting, though not unique. But to reach its western shore and discover the lake's outlet flowing through a gorge which led *into* the mountainside would, I am sure, have given the fathers of the subject apoplexy. My map had not prepared me for this. I came over a rise of land and eyed it suspiciously. Cormorants and bar-headed geese swam lazily on its languid waters, mocking my surprise. Reeds rustled in the wake of the tiny wavelets lapping the shore. A faint rumble came from the direction of the gorge. Otherwise, silence greeted me. In the whole of the basin surrounding this bizarre aberration of the landscape, I seemed at that moment to be the only human being.

I should have known better. Across the lake a rifle fired. Squinting, I could make out a group of figures, and wooden buildings half hidden among the pines. I had forgotten that RaRa Tal was a national park, and national parks have wardens. I stomped crossly round to the cluster of huts, introduced myself and signed in.

The park was guarded by forty-five bored soldiers. I couldn't imagine what they were guarding it against; I didn't ask. It was their rifle practice that had disturbed my peace across the lake. I found them playing cards. As I signed the visitors' book I noted with some surprise that I was their second guest of the month, my predecessor being a Dutchman called Pieter van Bergen op Zoom. Under the heading 'Purpose of Visit' he had written 'espionage'. I suppose after 'Pieter van Bergen op Zoom' he thought he had better put something the soldiers would understand.

A mile beyond the soldiers' encampment was the only other evidence of human endeavour at RaRa – a deserted village. Its people had been evicted, according to the wardens, because it had been decided they had no place in a national park. The government had therefore resettled them in the lowlands. Their fine houses and barley terraces, now collapsing, were a tribute to their triumph against the adversities of life at 10,000 feet in the Himalaya, and I reflected that it was a pity they hadn't enjoyed the same success against the bureaucrats of Kathmandu. The place was overgrown but somehow hospitable, as if the spirits of its last residents still walked its weed-ridden lanes and alleyways. I pitched my tent on a grassy patch by a sign which said, in faded Nepali, 'RARA POST OFFICE'.

It was 27 December, just a couple of nights before the full moon: a fortunate coincidence, because as I was preparing supper my torch gave a flicker and expired. Luckily I had brought several spare batteries, carefully sealed in a plastic bag. It was only after a great deal of fiddling with them that it dawned on me that it was the bulb that was at fault. Bulbs of this kind were almost certainly unobtainable west of Pokhara, and it hadn't occurred to me to bring another one. My supply of candles had long since been used up, so it looked very much as if I was going to have to spend the rest of my evenings in the dark.

The prospect of living a little more simply, of edging a little closer towards the freedom I had come to seek, of learning to live without one more convenience of the modern world, should have filled me with excitement. Just six months previously I had said that I wanted to see how the people here coped with their difficulties and misfortunes, and so perhaps gain some insight into how to handle my own life a little better. Now, halfway through the walk, I was as far from achieving this ambition as the day I had begun. True, the idea itself had been naïve: as if a few months' observation and reflection could wipe out a lifetime's conditioning. But I hadn't even given it a chance! There had been so many opportunities to let go of my Western heritage of aspirations, prejudice and greed; to open my mind to the evidence that was all around me of other ways of thought; for just once in my life to float free. I had let all these precious opportunities go. Now, as yet another chance to learn something from the walk was staring me in the face, the only blessing of torchlessness that I could think of was that I would no longer have to look at the horrible suppers of soup, rice and tsampa that had become my staple diet.

The moon cast an eerie light through the pines, picking out the shapes of the crumbling houses around me. Suddenly my senses were alerted. A human figure passed silently across the open space in front of me and entered a ruin to my right. A few seconds later the unmistakable yellow glow of an oil lamp came through the cracks between the stones.

I waited. Nothing happened. Five minutes passed. Still nothing. I rattled my saucepans. They echoed on the silent stones. I stumbled through the moonlight to the door of the ruin and looked in.

The man gazed up at me, still cross-legged from where his evening meditation had been so rudely interrupted by my saucepans. He showed no resentment at the intrusion, but as he bade me come in I felt his eyes searching me with more than the idle curiosity of a stranger. I squatted on a piece of ragged carpet and put my hands together in greeting. '*Namaskaar!*'

The meditant spoke excellent Nepali and greeted me profusely in return. He wore a new homespun robe dyed maroon, with wolf fur at the neck and wrist. On his feet were maroon felt boots. A thick fur hat covered his head. He looked too well dressed to be a simple hermit, but the sacks of food and can of cooking oil in a corner of the room suggested he was indeed some kind of recluse. There was no furniture to be seen, and no religious artifacts to suggest that he might have been a lama. After half an hour's conversation I had discovered only that he came from Gum Ghadi, a village not far to the east which he called by its Hindu name of Srinagar. This was odd, because he himself was a Buddhist. He told me this several times, as if he rarely had the opportunity to talk about it and was going to make the most of this one. I listened closely, picking up bits here and there as he held his forehead in thought and paraphrased the words of the Buddha. '*Never anticipate, never expect, never look forward, and above all, never look back. Never say "if only . . ."; never even think it. Concentrate on the present, because the past is dead, and the future, whatever it is, will not be what you were expecting it to be.*'

He shot me that same piercing look I had been conscious of as I entered the room. 'Of course,' he smiled, 'you will find this an unusual way of looking at things. I expect it is exactly the opposite to how you have been taught. You cannot concentrate just on the present and still expect to pass exams, go to college and get a good job. I am a miserable failure at these things because I have never in my whole life set myself goals.'

I ventured that my own goals didn't seem to be getting me anywhere at the moment.

'I know. I can see it in your eyes. You are full of doubts and self-pity. All the way from Pokhara you have been walking round in circles.' (I hadn't mentioned I had come from Pokhara.) 'You are on the point of giving up your goals because you think they have failed you; but in truth it is you who have failed your goals.'

He paused and repeated some of the words so that I could look them up, sheepishly, in my Nepali pocket dictionary.

'Do not abandon your goals. Just think carefully about the many different ways there are of achieving them. Consider too whether you should really try to achieve all of them. Some of your goals may turn out to be too difficult ever to achieve, or on reflection you may decide they are not worth achieving. Other goals may be worth devoting your whole life to.' He laughed. 'That last part is not the word of the Buddha, but you may find it suits your predicament.'

111

Suddenly he became brisk. 'Come, it is late. My lamp is burning low and I see you've had a tiring day. Sleep well. Tomorrow you must leave. The snows are coming and you have far to go.'

I slept fitfully. The wise man's discourse became interwoven with my own muddled feelings, and eventually these organised themselves into a dream where he was sitting by the water's edge, legs crossed, looking out across the lake under a full moon that, in reality, had yet to come. I approached from the ruined village and sat down beside him. For several minutes we listened to the lapping of the waves at our feet, the only sound in the mountain night. Then he broke the silence with the same words he had recited to me earlier. *'Concentrate on the present ... the past is dead ... and the future will not be what you were expecting it to be.'*

He spoke in a monotone, as if in a dream – which, of course, he was. I was aware of other people listening: many people. I could hear them moving closer behind us. I glanced round sharply but saw no one. I strained my eyes to see into the shadows beneath the trees; still no one. And when I turned back towards the lake, the wise man too was gone.

Dawn broke with low cloud hanging round the mountains and a gusty wind blowing off the lake. The water was grey and choppy. The meditant had disappeared, leaving only his sacks of food and can of cooking oil, looking ridiculously ordinary in the morning light. The soldiers were going unsmilingly about their chores. They faced long, grim weeks when they would be cut off from civilisation (if that is the way to describe Jumla). As I left their huts and headed west, the first snow-flakes began to fall.

I ran before the approaching blizzard, racing it down the gorge of the Khatyar Khola which drained RaRa Tal. Everything disappeared into the white mist. Time and again I stumbled along what I thought was the path, only to find myself on an abandoned barley terrace. The driving snow piled up on my pack and then on me, freezing in place so I became a walking snowman. My progress slowed as I weakened with the effort of pushing through the drifts. I picked my way for five hours through the blinding, dizzying storm, and finally camped in a riverside meadow – an absurd place considering the likely run-off from the snow, but the first flat ground I had come to in an hour of gathering dusk. In any case, I could physically go no further and I wasn't even sure if I was in the right valley.

But wait. The right valley? The *right* valley? What in hell was the right valley and what was so special about it that made it right? Was the right valley the one that led to my next goal? Or the one that would lead me out of the storm? Or this one, for the very reason that this was the one I happened to be in, and just at this moment, I had no choice. *Especially* because I had no choice. I peered through the gloom at the way I had come and saw that my footprints had already been covered by the driving snow. There was no question about it: I was stuck. And although I was cold, wet, exhausted and hungry my mind was clear. The goal was no longer fixed. I would accept whatever came.

I hammered the guy-ropes deep into a drift, crawled into my sodden sleeping bag and shivered myself to sleep.

7

Karnali

'All over the Himalayas it generally rains for
a few days towards the end of December.'
John Morris, *A Winter in Nepal*

Diary, 29 December 1982
Waiting for a dawn that never comes. Watching for signs
from my sleeping bag, I feel anticipation turning slowly
to resignation: the helplessness of a passenger waiting for
a cancelled train. I have no idea what time it is; my watch
is lying in a pool of melted snow at the bottom of my
pack. My inner clock says it ought to be getting light, but
nothing seems to penetrate the inky blackness, and I write
blind. The blizzard is still tearing at the trees above my
head, but it is a distant sound, muffled, as if from far
away. I can't understand it. Everything seems so far
away.

On an impulse I put my notebook aside and reached out
towards the side of the tent. To my horror my hand hit
something solid. Beyond the flysheet was a wall of snow. I was
buried.

I unzipped the tent-flaps and scrabbled. Mercifully the
snow was still quite soft and I reached the surface in less than a
minute. As I had expected, it was broad daylight – or as broad
as it could be in the middle of a snowstorm. I could just make
out the shapes of the pines, their branches prettily festooned
like a monstrous Christmas card. The tent seemed to be acting
as a trap for the snow which was funnelling down the valley;
as far as I could see, very little was landing on the valley sides.

114

But it was difficult to judge with so much still swirling around me. I did a little more digging, just enough to make sure I wouldn't get buried again, then dived back inside.

Two things were clear. One, I had chosen a bloody awful campsite: two, it was going to be my home for a while. I wriggled into my still sodden sleeping bag and made some tea.

I had never spent a whole day alone before. Writing this now, months later, I find it difficult to believe that the prospect actually worried me. Solitude is easy. Far from being frightening, it is a luxury featherbed constantly tempting me into its embracing folds – and like Oscar Wilde, I can resist everything except temptation.

In spite of all my weeks travelling, however, I had yet to learn the difference between solitude and loneliness. I understood loneliness, that dark void that creeps up when one is, or feels, far from friends. I had experienced this already many times on the trip – paradoxically most of all when surrounded by people, for example in Delhi, in Varanasi and in Kathmandu. And that should have provided the clue, because loneliness is a need not for people, but for the right people; a desire not for company, but for the company of loved ones. Yet in my ignorance I still confused the two, and the prospect of a complete day in this small snowbound tent seemed fraught with misery.

Sipping from my chipped enamel mug, I gazed listlessly through my tent-flaps. The snow had eased but the sky was still leaden, the world silent and grey. After all the colours and sounds I had become used to it was like watching black and white television with the volume off.

To lift my spirits I put myself to work. The tent had started to disappear again and I set out to excavate a trench right round it, using my ice-axe as a pick for the hard snow and as a shovel for the softer parts. Then I cleared a path to the river-bank, so I could get water that wasn't frozen. All this took a considerable amount of effort, and I fell back into the tent with a sense of something achieved. I ate some tsampa and drank some more tea and decided (since I still didn't know the time) to call it breakfast. Now that I had established some sort of pattern to the day, I felt much better. I settled back and picked up my last remaining reading matter: a tattered and mildewed copy of *A Winter in Nepal*, John Morris's vintage work, which had caught my eye in one of Kathmandu's secondhand bookshops. 'All over the Himalayas,' it assured me confidently, 'it generally rains for a few days towards the end of December ...'

I was not halfway through the book when it began to grow dark. I had been lost in the Nepal of the 1950s, when the Nepalese still worshipped pumpkins as symbols of fertility and railway tickets (of all things) as symbols of safe and speedy delivery in childbirth. It was also a time when table manners had not yet become a thing of the past. 'Appreciation of a meal is expressed by belching, but to break wind otherwise in the presence of others is to proclaim oneself a boor.' Reluctantly, as the approaching dusk made it difficult to see the pages, I put aside this splendid tome and looked out.

It was not at all as I expected. In the few hours I had been reading the snow had stopped, the sky had cleared and stars had come out over a landscape that had turned from grey to luminous white. The day I had feared so much was over, and with it the blizzard. I had hardly noticed either of them pass.

Next morning I was up at dawn. The snow had formed a hard crust overnight and I wanted to make some progress before it melted in the morning sun. Now that the cloud had lifted, the path was much easier to follow and I even found some footprints for a few hundred yards, leading to a stream. Their owner had been barefoot. During the morning I passed some huts with a welter of human and animal prints round their doors; but they were shut and bolted. A teenage girl, bare-armed and barefoot, grimaced as she ploughed her way to fetch water from a well. An older woman saw me, yanked her shawl across her face and hurried on. I came to a hamlet in which the villagers stared sullenly at me from their doorsteps. Even the smallest children failed to smile. The cheerfulness and vigour that I had come to take for granted had gone with the storm.

Grey clouds returned in the afternoon, threatening more

snow. But I was descending steeply now, and by the time it caught up with me it had become a sleety drizzle, neither snow nor rain, which drove pockmarks into the snow underfoot and then turned it to slush. I pitched my tent on a patch of bare ground by the river I had been following, which I hoped was the Khatyar Khola. For some reason my butane stove refused to light. Idiotically, instead of taking a few minutes to dry it out and unblock the jet, I threw it aside and began collecting brushwood for a fire. Naturally the sticks were soaked. I got through a whole box of matches and a bevy of curses before I gave up the doomed task and retired, frustrated and supperless, to my still damp sleeping bag.

So obsessed was I with my pyrotechnics that I completely overlooked the possibility that the river might rise in the night. Considering how much snow had melted in its catchment area that day, it was a wonder it didn't carry me off to the Karnali. Well before first light I was woken by its roar. The surging water was throwing up gusts of wind which grabbed my flysheet like a playful puppy. Drugged by sleep, I crawled out to find the river a good six feet above its earlier level, and lapping voraciously at my guy-ropes. It was skedaddle or be swamped. Again I cursed, but more inwardly this time because I couldn't help feeling it was no less than I deserved. Noah Pilkington, caught napping with an unfinished ark, had been spared the Flood.

I stumbled on — bedraggled, drowsy and quite possibly lost. My map, in another of its flights of fancy, showed paths and villages all around. I scanned the mountainsides for both in vain. I was running short of food, and my earlier nonchalance about knowing where I was seemed now like bravado I could hardly afford. If this valley I was blundering down turned out *not* to belong to the Khatyar Khola, I might be in trouble.

Late in the day I met a lone porter, a Pahaari Hindu on his way to Gum Ghadi on a mission for the Governor of Mugu. Like me, he was happy to see another human being. He plied me with the usual questions — where was I going, where had I come from, would I like to sell my boots — then broached the

one that just a few days previously I had been asking everybody else: 'How far is it to RaRa Tal?'

I had absolutely no idea what distance I had covered in the
blizzard, but was ashamed to admit I didn't know. Almost
without thinking I gave him the usual reply. 'Oh, about four
kos I suppose.'

'That's what I thought,' he nodded wisely.

I offered him a moist cigarette from a pack I had picked up
in Jumla. As I helped him light it, I noticed a fresh marigold in
his hair and complimented him on it.

'You'll find lots more down the valley,' he smiled. 'The
Khatyar Khola is famous for them.'

'This is the Khatyar Khola?'

'Of course. It's the daughter of *Karnali-aamaa*, mother of
all rivers, which you'll reach tomorrow.' He looked at me
curiously. 'Didn't you know?'

Snow still clothed the valley's upper slopes, and remained in
occasional wet patches right down to the river. In a bizarre
juxtaposition it even adorned the fronds of some wayside
banana plants. But by nightfall I was out of it and walking at
last on dry ground. I carried on by moonlight beneath wild
walnut trees. Seeing a lighted house, I knocked and asked if I
could buy some food, hoping the woman would understand
my Nepali. It was a vain hope. She shouted back angrily in a
strange brogue, her gold nose-rings jangling in wrath. I
blurted my apologies and withdrew to pitch my tent on what
later turned out to be her potato patch. After a while her
husband emerged, all smiles, and chatted at great length in the
same incomprehensible tongue, squatting by my tent-flaps.
He seemed to be asking me to pardon his wife's unseemly
behaviour, and ended up presenting me, as if in recompense,
with a clay dish of buffalo yogurt. He didn't mention the
potatoes, tactful man, and I slept in happy ignorance of them
till morning.

High on a ridge above the confluence of the Khatyar Khola
and the Karnali, looking like a transplanted Mezzogiorno hill

118

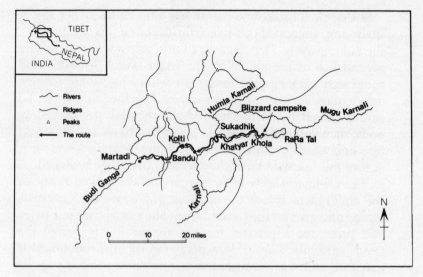

6   RaRa Tal to Martadi

village, sat the huddle of houses called Sukadhik. I arrived in
the village square and was, as usual, surrounded. The hubbub
was deafening; everybody wanted to talk to the strange
apparition. Children fingered my pack, dogs sniffed my boots,
and the village policeman, quite bewildered by it all, inter-
rogated me with what I can only suppose was intended to be
brisk efficiency. After the days on my own it was nice to be
with these lively folk. I stood and absorbed the colours, the
movement, the smell of bodies, the smell of animal dung.
Then my nose recognised the smell of cooking and I remembered I was hungry. I asked if there was any chance of some
food. Of course, said six voices at once.

After some argument I was taken to a clifftop house and
introduced to a graceful woman who appeared to be the
great-grandmother of the village. I stood in her stone-flagged
courtyard, flanked by a giant sunflower on my left and a
purple bougainvillaea, in full bloom even at this late season,
on my right. The village odours were at once masked by the
heady scent of the flowers, and the woman waved me to sit
between them as she set rice and vegetables to cook.

She worked briskly, so that it was difficult to tell her age. A slight limp suggested possible arthritis, but if this troubled her she hid it bravely. Her elegance of movement was matched by a prudence of tongue. With the single word 'Maake?' and some sign language she asked if I would like some roasted maize to take with me on my journey. I nodded hesitantly. To assure herself that I understood she showed me the yellow pods, then without further ado proceeded to roast them on an iron hob which straddled the fire, tossing them back and forth across the hotplate until they were thoroughly browned. A pair of grindstones lay in the corner and she barked at one of the children to watch the cooking pot while she sat cross-legged and ground the roasted corn. She sieved the flour twice and presented a plateful for my approval. I inspected the result carefully, like a Homepride flourman, pronounced it first rate and was rewarded with a radiant, toothless smile. With deft fingers the woman wrapped the flour in a banana leaf, securing it with a strand of liana which she tied with a neat bow. The whole operation had taken less than a quarter of an hour.

A mile below its confluence with the Khatyar Khola, deep in a wind-sculpted gorge, the Karnali is crossed by one of the few suspension bridges in west Nepal, strung between two rocky promontories jutting into the river. As I zigzagged down and crossed its rattling planks the sun made a belated appearance, shining straight up the canyon from low in the south-west. The strata on the canyon walls threw up a thousand reflections, wet rock glistening red. It made me nervous. In this arid chasm where cacti grew, the water left everywhere by the recent storm seemed somehow ominous, as if portending some dreadful climatic change.

I followed the Karnali into the lightshow, noticing how its colour seemed to change at every turn. Its roar made an appropriate soundtrack. A troupe of langur monkeys, each the size of a human, chattered among the rocks above my head where they had taken shelter from the storm. They stared down insolently, daring me to come closer, and when I did, loped easily away over precipices that would have defied a mountain goat.

A New Year's Eve moon rose into a sky that was at last clear of stormclouds. I walked on. The rocky outcrops which less than an hour previously had been an angry blood-red now glowed white and tranquil as I wound beneath them. At night the countryside seemed to take on a new personality. Flowers gave off heady perfumes in the rapidly cooling air, and the canyon walls threw up patches of mist which drifted aimlessly among the pinnacles and buttes. Engulfed for a minute by one of these earthbound clouds, I was disoriented and stood motionless for fear of stepping over the edge. Then the curtain was plucked away and the ghostly canyon reappeared: white rocks reflecting a white moon, with the river a white ribbon in the blackness below.

Moon and stars had long moved on from their familiar early evening positions when at last I pitched camp under a pipal tree. They flooded my campsite with surreal brilliance in the clear night air. The river's roar was muted here – almost soothing – and the luminous rocks were all around, protecting me.

'*Namaste!*'

It was morning, and a clutch of boyish faces were grinning into the tent. From the bags they carried it was obvious they were on their way to school. The sun was already high and I admonished myself for being caught off guard. I also admonished the boys, using some choice phrases not widely known outside Yorkshire – predictably to no effect.

I never quite got used to being a superstar. Whenever I stopped for the night, people would pop up from nowhere to feast their eyes on the white-hot technology I carried: tent, gas stove, sleeping bag, dud torch, boots. Whenever I passed a group of houses, young and old alike would stop what they were doing and start trotting along behind me, often for miles. Sometimes they would ask questions about how much this, that or the other piece of clothing cost; sometimes they were happy just to stare at my retreating bum. Today, the children whispered excitedly to each other, working out scintillating questions for the sahib in their pidgin English. 'Your countree-a population – what *eez*?' At first this one baffled me, but I made a wild guess in the hope that, as with the cost of my clothes, any figure with more than three noughts would do. From across the fields came a cry, and an older boy came running. Oh good, I thought, some intelligent conversation. He came up panting as if being chased by a tiger. 'How-a old are you-a?' My heart sank.

I set off down the valley like a mother duck, gathering a few more children at every house. The adults laughed, and a few joined in the crocodile. An old man leapt up from under a tree, yelling. He had no hands, and waved his stumpy arms angrily at me. He was asking for money. In much of Asia as in Africa and parts of Latin America, people use their disabilities as instruments for begging. The more ghastly the affliction, the more ferociously they beg – as if a few rupees, takas or bahts would give them back their lost limbs. In Calcutta, parents have even been known to break their children's arms and legs to improve their begging efficiency. My followers had no sympathy for the man, shouting back rudely and lobbing stones at him. I joined in the hullabaloo with some drivel of my own and carried on, guilty and ashamed that I hadn't had the guts at least to stop and talk to him. But I was under the critical eyes of my crocodile. They showed no such soft emotions and peeled off merrily to school.

At the village of Bandu I left the Karnali and started up towards the pass which led to the Budi Ganga. Almost immediately I came upon a great commotion. Against a giant banyan tree were propped two dozen loaded wicker dokos. The rumpus was coming from their owners: two dozen Hindu porters who were noisily engaged in cooking and consuming a great meal. The banyan shaded a *chautaara* – a long bench of stones, carefully carved and positioned so that porters could set down their cargoes with a minimum of effort to rest and eat. Chautaaras are found throughout Nepal, and no one who has travelled on foot in that country has not at some time sunk gratefully onto one. Almost every steep hill has a chautaara at the top; indeed, knowing this is sometimes all that keeps one climbing.

The chautaara at Bandu happened to have a tea-house nearby, so provided shade, rest and sustenance – all a traveller might need. In function if not in appearance it was very like the truckstops which are such a characteristic feature of North American roads. In place of the jukebox a man was strumming a two-chord melody on a saarangi. In place of those jolly highway songs that belt out of every truckstop jukebox, one of the porters was accompanying the musician in a fine baritone voice, venting similar sentiments in the form of the lyrics to a well-known Nepalese travelling song. In place of boloney-on-rye with side salad there was lentils-on-rice with soggy cabbage. And in just the same way that truck drivers fastidiously check their vehicles, tightening a rope here and a knot there, so the porters pored over their dokos, adjusting loads and comparing each other's weights. To complete the picture, four of them were sitting in the dirt playing cards.

Unlike their North American counterparts, many Nepalese chautaaras are several centuries old. When a chautaara is completed it is 'consecrated' by planting two sacred fig trees: *Ficus benghalensis*, the banyan, and *Ficus religiosa*, the pipal. These trees have a lifespan of several hundred years, yet often, as here at Bandu, one or the other has long since died. From the girth of the surviving one I guessed that the Bandu chautaara had been there since at least the sixteenth century.

The porters were in good spirits and gave me a rousing cheer as I passed. (Nelapese truckstops, it seems, still serve beer.) Immediately the path steepened. I passed a *chorten*, a whitewashed stone shrine garlanded with marigolds and coloured streamers, an indication that I was coming to a difficult bit. Chortens, like the wooden effigies I had found protecting the bridge over the Uttar Ganga, are maintained by Buddhist travellers to ward off the demons that haunt particularly formidable sections; the more trimmings, the more demons. This one also had a bell, so that those who wished could warn the demons of their approach. Timid travellers, believing that there were demons behind every bush, hang streamers from trees when there is no chorten around: a pretty sight, especially in winter. I rang the bell once, loudly, and started up.

The snow on this pass was wet and dirty, but the porters coming the other way had stamped out a trail of sorts. At the village of Kolti, incredibly, I found an airstrip being built on a hillside ledge. Gangs of men were breaking rocks in the snow and carrying sackfuls of the resulting gravel to make the runway. The work had obviously been going on for some time, because weeds had taken over one end of the runway and they hadn't finished the other end yet. I secretly rather hoped they never would. Aircraft would admittedly bring much needed improvements to the valley; I was sure they would be welcomed by everyone except possibly the porters whom they would make redundant. But they would also bring with them a sophistication, a touch of city life, which I felt irrationally but insistently had no place here.

Ploughing upwards, slipping and falling every few yards, I realised how much I had deteriorated since Jumla. The pass was only 9,000 feet, but my lungs and muscles were behaving as if it were twice as high. My feet were sore, hips bruised by the pressure of the rucksack, hair tangled, face filthy. My clothes were in shreds; and now, just when I had got them dry, they were getting soaked again. I wanted to stand under a hot shower, drink wine, eat cheese, sunbathe, read books, listen to music, be with friends. Sunk in misery, I stumbled on, but even reaching the summit failed to cheer me up.

As a place to be depressed in, the Budi Ganga valley around Martadi is singularly fitting. Like most of west Nepal's valleys it was once thickly forested with spruce and blue pine, but this is difficult to imagine now. The demand for firewood has stripped all the accessible slopes of conifers, and the need for ever more animal fodder has mauled the few remaining oak. Agricultural land is in short supply, and I was glad to see that many of the denuded areas had been terraced for cultivation. Where for some reason they hadn't, erosion of the exposed soil had ensured that they never would. The problem is endemic throughout the Himalaya – not, as is commonly believed, just in those parts where trekkers make additional demands. Perhaps it was because of my own wretched state that I noticed it particularly here.

Martadi is an expanding centre for the Bajura district, which appeared to be administered from some corrugated iron sheds behind the school. I dumped my pack in the 'hotel' and sloshed through the village's slovenly streets. Grubby youngsters extended filthy hands – the first begging by children I had encountered since the Kali Gandaki – while their mothers watched impassively from their doorsteps.

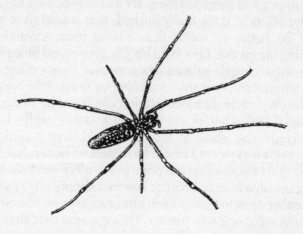

During the night, as I lay listening to the screaming infants in the room next door, I thought as so often in the previous few days of my RaRa friend. What would he have made of this devastated landscape and its sullen inhabitants? Buddhists attach a considerable significance to acts of creation or destruction. Whatever the results, they maintain that the acts themselves are neither right nor wrong; good and evil are not inherent in things but merely qualities we project on to them. A good philosophy to apply to screaming infants. The Buddha would have seen these particular ones simply for what they were, which was part of the resident community of Martadi's hotel – no more or less. The children didn't see anything wrong with making this infernal din. Neither did their mother and father, who I noticed had now joined in. In just the same way, I had to admit, I rarely used to think twice about playing my Bob Marley records even though my neighbours hated Bob Marley and would have much preferred a spot of Bach. And so, throughout the world, one person's joy is another's headache.

If you can't put a definitive value on the creation of things, then it follows that you can't measure the value of their destruction either. The washed-out mountainsides of the Budi Ganga were inherently no better or worse than the conifer-clad slopes that preceded them. If I had snapped my fingers and the family next door had vanished, that would have been in itself no better or worse than having them screaming and keeping me awake. Or would it? The spruce and blue pine had supported a fragile balance of interwoven lives – plant, insect, bird, animal and human – extending far beyond the confines of the forest. Surely their obliteration could not be so curtly dismissed? And what if the screaming family really had disappeared? The whole of Martadi would have mourned, and for what it was worth I would have slept no better than before. In the end I suspect that it is pointless to place one's own judgement on such events, because however deeply one might wish it, neither creation nor destruction can ever be reversed. The Buddha went one step further. He suggested that all incidents should be accepted simply as products of the passage of time.

Of course, human beings have been busily putting judgements on things since the world began. We have put endless effort into creating 'good' and destroying 'evil'. Recently, in their enthusiasm to be able to destroy an 'evil' enemy with weapons they call deterrents, the superpowers have possibly managed to engineer the destruction of the whole world. Individuals often feel helpless in the face of such monumental forces – as indeed we are. But I do think there is a way that we can still strive in the things we do to achieve a quality that can be judged independently, a quality that is real in the existentialist sense. All we have to do is try to limit our impact on other people and things.

This is really rather old fashioned. As far as *things* are concerned, pundits have been pushing the idea of minimum impact for years. They call themselves environmentalists. But I have never heard anyone suggest that we should also try to limit our impact on *people*, by keeping ourselves more to ourselves and not trying to influence others quite so much. Taken literally, this could lead to an apocalyptic decline of the human species because we would have scarcely any intercourse, social or physical. This might be going rather too far. But Martadi did provide me with the seed of an idea which is quite similar to one of the basic premises of Taoism: that is, that we should perhaps think a bit more carefully before following our impulses to talk, write, persuade, buy, steal, kill, promote ourselves, reproduce ourselves or fiddle with the natural environment. In the words of the Tao, we should refrain from any activity contrary to nature. Although the Chinese call this idea *wu-wei* or 'non-action', it does not mean doing nothing, but rather allowing other people and things to do what they do naturally, 'so that their nature will be satisfied'. Working in this way, we could limit many of our more aggressive actions against people and nature and would have the gratification of knowing that we were not causing any more damage than was absolutely necessary. This would still be far from Nirvana, the ultimate peace, which could only come with the condition of neither creating nor destroying: that is, not existing at all. But we are all doomed to exist – the crowd in the room next door, just as much as me lying in my sleeping bag listening to them. So one should perhaps simply keep as low a profile, within reason, as one can.

With this thought I resisted the temptation to go round and add my own ranting and raving to the pandemonium next door. Instead I settled down to meditate. I chose my subject and concentrated hard until I was only dimly aware of the babble, then allowed myself to drift into unconsciousness. At least this assured me of some sleep. But it failed to pull me out of the pits, and the cowbells which woke me in the morning seemed even more tuneless than usual.

8

Beyond the Budi Ganga

'If anything can go wrong, it will.'
Arthur Bloch, *Murphy's Law*

Hard times bring out either the best or the worst in one. They raise you to new heights of understanding – or they tear you to bits. From Martadi onwards the walk was by no stretch of the imagination a happy one. The land seemed pillaged by a combination of greed and ignorance, leaving nothing but landslides, barren slopes and stone-choked gulleys. In truth, the ignorance was mine. Much of this destruction had happened during an earthquake in 1966, and the deforestation since then had been part of a grim effort to replace the farmland lost. But walking through the wreckage I never imagined there might be mitigating circumstances; I saw only the changes in the landscape and they made me immeasurably sad.

The people around me were changing too; I had become used to the good-humoured Thakuri, Bhotia and Tibetan people and was not at all prepared for the aloof Brahmins of the far west. Brahmins are Hindus of the highest caste – the caste of priests. In towns and cities many of them have broadened their traditional outlook and occupy positions as civil servants, teachers and businessmen. But in the hills they remain more orthodox – not necessarily working as priests, but abiding strictly by the rules of their caste in matters of eating, touching, working and marrying. The rules are aimed at minimising contact with people of other – that is, lower – castes. Being outside the caste system did not exempt me from this treatment. I tried not to take their prickliness personally (after all, they were only doing what I had been advocating myself at the hotel at Martadi) but I can't pretend it didn't affect me. I was clearly seen as an intruder; I felt like one; and eventually I began to behave like one.

But it would be churlish to blame the Brahmins for all my woes. I felt very weak by now, walking at less than half the pace I had set in the Kali Gandaki basin, and suffering, as they say in the motor trade, from excessive wear and tear. My knees were excruciatingly painful, especially on the steep downhill sections of which there were still many. Most ominous of all, over the past few days I had developed a loud cracking sound in my hip. Thankfully this peculiar affliction only made itself heard every few hundred yards, but it was growing steadily more frequent and I had visions of finishing the walk ticking away like the crocodile in *Peter Pan*. It would happen completely without warning, usually when I was being followed by a procession of kids, and would be accompanied by a stab of pain in my thigh and a ripple of laughter down the line.

Since meeting the meditant at RaRa Tal I had also become increasingly aware that my hopes for the walk were not being fulfilled – could never be fulfilled, because they had been based on the ridiculous proposition that by immersing myself for a few months in a harsh environment, I would learn how to cope with physical hardships and by analogy with the more metaphysical problems of my own life. I was not the first to be seduced by this fallacy, and I don't suppose for a moment I shall be the last. It is a romantic notion which has the added attraction of a certain amount of logic. But I think the real motive for many adventurers who claim this as their justification is the simple, unadorned urge to run away. It was certainly so with me. This realisation now, so late in my so-called adventure, was rather difficult to swallow.

From the Budi Ganga I had to traverse one more major river basin – the Seti – and cross one more watershed before coming down to the Mahakali which, since 1816, has formed Nepal's western frontier with India. I left Martadi with the usual

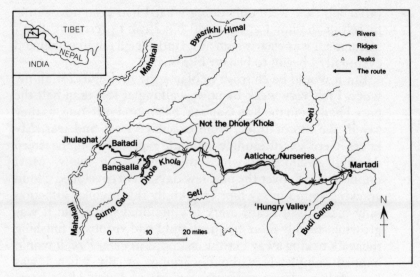

7   Martadi to Jhulaghat

procession and crossed the tributary I had been following on a
bright new suspension bridge, planks rattling and steel cables
glinting in the morning sun. An hour later I was crossing the
Budi Ganga itself, then two hours' hard climbing brought me
to a notch in an otherwise continuous 8,000 foot ridge from
which I could look out over the valley of another tributary
flowing in from the west. It was a wide valley and for once it
seemed to be shown on the map. However it was not named,
and after an hour descending its northern flanks, looking
unsuccessfully for something for lunch, I decided to call it
Hungry Valley.

The people of Hungry Valley were Thakuris, not Brahmins,
and would have done a good trade catering for travellers if
they had had anything to sell. The few fields that had not been
washed away looked impoverished, as if they had already
been squeezed of any fertility they might once have had. I
passed two villages and noticed how poorly maintained the
houses were: corners crumbling, with gaping holes in the thin
straw roofs. Some villagers directed me to a tea-house but it

130

was locked and shuttered. Dangling in the breeze was a handwritten sign in Devanagari script – saying, no doubt, 'Closed until further notice'. I stomped on.

Every few hundred yards the path had been swept away by landslides, some of them ancient and colonised by weeds, others recent and raw. The freshest of all, possibly caused by the same storm that had caught me at RaRa Tal, had exposed a layer of the most extraordinary bright purple rock. Streaks of dazzling scree from this latest scar spilled down the mountainside, as if the earth was bleeding from a freshly opened wound – which in a sense it was. Rounding a corner I came upon a complete ox skeleton lying across the path where it had fallen from above. It had been there for months and would presumably remain there until it turned to dust. No one would dream of moving or stepping over such sacred bones, and a path had been worn in a reverent semicircle around it.

In the late afternoon, under a leaden sky that threatened another storm, I arrived at the Artichoke Nurseries. At least that's what the name sounded like. The nurserymen took me in just as the first wave of heavy rain began. They sat me in front of a brazier and I steamed like a plum pudding. At first they merely asked the usual questions –then, seeing my sorry state, insisted I stay the night. I didn't need much persuading; the thought of artichokes for supper had already crossed my hungry mind. Much to my disappointment, however, it turned out that not a single solitary artichoke was being cultivated among the apple and pear trees the men were nursing, and they explained rather apologetically that at the Aatichor Nurseries supper usually consisted of rice and lentils. Ah well, it had been a nice thought. I sat back, still steaming slightly in imitation of the cooking pot in front of me, and listened to their smalltalk.

Nepal, west of the Karnali, has more in common with the adjacent Himalayan parts of India than with the rest of Nepal. In the seventeenth century, as the Malla kings were consolidating their hold on the Kathmandu Valley, they had already lost the far west to the Katyur rulers of Kumaon in what is now northern Uttar Pradesh. The true events of this turbulent and heroic period have now been lost in legend. For example, it is said that a certain Nepalese soldier named Sangram Karki, stationed in the mountains between the Budi Ganga and the Seti, made off with a caravan of elephants laden with salt, horses laden with precious textiles and goats laden with gold coins – no less – and delivered them to the Katyur king. The creep. Throughout the nineteenth century and into the twentieth the people of this part of Nepal looked to India for their trade, religion, culture, architecture and art. It was hardly surprising, therefore, that I found these nurserymen speaking a dialect closer to Hindi than Nepali; so different from that I had learned in Kathmandu and, as in Jumla, I had the greatest difficulty in following what was being said.

Dressed in the Kumaoni costume of baggy striped trousers and multicoloured topis, the nurserymen looked for all the world as if they were on their way to a fancy-dress party. In between bouts of animated discussion (mostly about the price of pears) we took turns to smoke from a great brass hookah, inhaling by means of a curly pipe which drew the smoke through a water filter. I found this much more enjoyable than talking. The water cooled the smoke so I could draw it in without burning my throat, and the contraption soon started to emit a soothing bubbling sound, like those old television programmes by Hans and Lotte Hass.

Supper was served on shiny brass plates, with bowls of honey to be poured on the remainder of the rice when the lentils had gone. Entrée, main course and dessert, all in one. Afterwards, to avoid further conversation, I toyed with the nurserymen's transistor radio, tuning in to Chinese stations which, if equally unintelligible, at least didn't demand audience participation. Turning the dial, I was startled to hear the measured tones of the BBC World Service – instantly recognisable, even through the static. I closed my eyes and was transported back to the days of the Ovaltinies and ITMA, when presenters wore bow ties and spoke through big bulbous microphones. You may have noticed that very occasionally the World Service forgets that those days have now gone, and I happened to catch it during one of these brief lapses. The static enhanced the effect splendidly. I sat back and indulged in ten minutes of pure fantasy, until one of the nurserymen (to save his batteries, no doubt) pointed to a corner and put his hands together to one cheek in a gesture of sleep. Like a child I wriggled and squirmed, begging for five minutes more, but like a father he patted me on the head and gently put the radio aside. I curled up where he indicated and was out like a light.

With the dawn came blue skies and a fresh breeze; a morning of rich aromas from the hedgerows, brought out by the night's downpour. The gardens of the houses had turned into lakes, but there were smiles and cheerful greetings as the sun dried out sodden animals, clothes and people. '*Namaste sahib*! – Hello sir!' A rare morning when I answered the inevitable questions about how much my various articles of clothing cost patiently and truthfully. It occurred to me that it might be worth while putting price tags on the more popular items.

I crossed a low pass into yet another valley, this one draining to the Seti which I would follow for the next few days. In remarkable contrast to Hungry Valley, the tea-houses here were open and doing a roaring trade. As well as providing a service for travellers they also formed a social centre for each village, where the men came to talk, knit and drink endless cups of tea. At one tea-house I came upon at sunset, more than twenty men were crammed on to three small benches, knitting needles clicking, gossiping away for all the world like a mothers' union.

Just when I thought things might at last be looking up, there followed a day of havoc, wreaked mainly by my smudged, dog-eared and accursed map which put the Seti ten miles too far west. The tributary I was following drained into a much larger stream which the cartographer had apparently chosen to ignore. This hardly surprised me; I had already lost any faith in this individual on the Sama Khola. Confident that I must eventually reach the Seti, I marched off down the river's left bank.

Some hours later a chance remark from one of the children in my procession made me look at the map afresh. I questioned the boy closely, straining to understand his thick dialect. Eventually I had to accept the awful truth, that this *was* the Seti; that I was on the wrong side of it; and that I had passed the one and only bridge several miles upstream. Everyone seemed to agree that there were no ferries, and swimming or wading was out of the question. A joker asked if I could walk on the water and got a thunderous glare in reply. There was nothing else for it but to retrace my steps to the bridge.

A band of cheerful Tibetans making camp by the wayside consoled me with sympathy and yak-butter tea served in an exquisite red wooden cup. They were going south to pick up rice from the plains. They sat cross-legged round their campfire, chubby faces grinning at me from the folds of their great homespun cloaks.

I explained to the Tibetans, as best I could, where I had come from and where I was trying to go. Amazingly, they understood. They agreed that my map was rotten, and that I should have crossed the bridge. They also told me that the way I had been intending to take to Baitadi and the Indian frontier was *na chaltiko* – 'not fashionable' – because of a difficult high altitude stretch. They showed me, on one of the less pulped sections of the map, another route which they reckoned was longer but 'more popular'.

I set out without delay to retrace the prints of these good Samaritans' rope soles, but failed to make the bridge by nightfall. I hardly had the energy to put up the tent. As usual a small crowd gathered in the twilight to watch the show. As usual I told them to clear off. This time, to my surprise, they did. Perhaps, I speculated, there was after all an ancient linguistic link between Yorkshire and this remote pocket of Asia?

At the bottom of my food bag was some so-called French onion soup that I had picked up in Kathmandu. It looked very sorry for itself. It had never seen France, but it had seen an awful lot of Nepal by now, and I decided to eat it before the rats did. Some potatoes I had been given went the same way. Potatoes are 90 per cent water, and therefore very silly things to hump over 10,000 foot passes. Predictably this strange feast made me violently ill, but I awoke the next morning feeling much better for it.

One of the reasons why I so often had a crocodile of followers was that nobody would ever, ever overtake me. It is part of the unwritten highway code of the Himalaya that to pass a sahib going in the same direction as oneself is a mark of the greatest disrespect; therefore the sedate sahib always has a procession in tow. I was, needless to say, the most dilatory traveller on the road, and my caravan sometimes reached ceremonial proportions – rather like the queues behind those other caravans one sees being towed by ageing Rovers around the roads of Britain.

At the Seti this problem became acute – not because there were a great many wayfarers about, but because I had virtually ground to a halt. I could barely summon the energy, either to keep moving or even, sometimes, to watch where I was putting my feet. Time and again I would stumble on the edge of a precipice, the weight of my pack almost toppling me over the rim, while my companions looked on in horror. I was running out of physical and spiritual steam; a heavy vehicle with a wide load, trundling along with the driver asleep. I was becoming a nuisance to others and a danger to myself.

Of course, I should have stopped: holed up for a few days and pampered myself a bit. But the momentum of the walk had become irresistible. However slow and painful it was, I had to go on. My progress was helped to a certain extent by my predilection for walking into the night, which continued even though there was now no moon. I did this partly to avoid sightseers, and partly because decent campsites never seemed to crop up when I wanted them. Fortunately in the clear west Nepal air I could find my way easily by starlight, and I had become so familiar with the quirks of my dear Blacks tent that I could put it up, so to speak, in pitch dark.

I had abandoned any idea of following the paths marked on the map. Rivers and mountains were turning up miles from where they should have been. When I showed the map to local people they scratched their heads in bewilderment, and no

wonder. It bore as much resemblance to this part of Nepal as
to the moon.

Two days after my inadvertent excursion down the Seti I
was lost again. The nearest town shown was Baitadi, some
fifteen miles to the west, but when I asked people about this
they gesticulated vaguely over the mountains, indicating that
it was a long way in a direction they weren't quite sure of. My
hopes of reaching Nepal's western frontier were receding – as
apparently was the frontier itself.

Perhaps I was going round in circles? But no, the rising and
setting sun assured me that I was indeed walking west. Therefore, I told myself, sooner or later I must reach the frontier and
India. Somehow, surrounded as I was by strange unmapped
mountains, the logic was not convincing.

The day I had anticipated walking down a deep valley I
found myself on a ridge of rolling hills covered with powdery
snow. In other circumstances it would have been breathtak-
ing. On the northern horizon was a formidable barrier of ice
and rock which could only have been the Byasrikhi Himal –
the group of 20,000 foot peaks where Nepal, Tibet and India
meet. But to the south, east and west, nothing was recognisable. I clambered down into a ravine which a shepherd told
me contained the source of the Dhole Khola. Here at least was
a river that was shown on my map; it flowed due west to the
Mahakali and the frontier. The only trouble was – as I
discovered the next day – the river I was following flowed
south.

I began to suspect a conspiracy. 'Is this the Dhole Khola?' I
asked everyone.

'*Ho, yo Dhole Khola ho!*' they replied in their strange
accents.

'Are you sure?'

'*Hajur!*'

And smiling sweetly, they would continue on their way.

Eventually I forced myself to sit down, brew some tea and
try to puzzle it out. No map could be so completely wrong as
this. It just wasn't possible. Very carefully, so it wouldn't
disintegrate, I spread out the rogue dyeline on a patch of grass

and weighted it down with stones. Then I looked at it, and the problem, from all possible angles.

The answer came to me in a flash of intuition halfway through my second cup of tea. I was indeed following the Dhole Khola. Everybody said so. The map showed the Dhole Khola flowing west. My Dhole Khola was flowing south. It was obvious. The mapmaker had simply put the name *Dhole Khola* on the wrong river. Far from heading westwards to the Mahakali, I had spent the day walking southwards to the Surna Gad.

I sat looking into my teacup, devastated. A youth came up and asked me how much my boots cost. I yelled at him. He made himself scarce. In reality the situation was not all that bad: an extra day's walking, a few more miles, another pass. But in my sickly state I couldn't cope with it. It was more than an hour before I could summon the strength to move.

I retraced my steps to a point where a track turned west up a pine-clad tributary valley. I had to ford the Dhole Khola to reach it, and slithered and skated on the slippery stones like a grotesque ballet dancer. For once my Bolivian stick method failed me and I got two ice-cold dunkings. But a band of Pahaari porters on the other side confirmed that this was indeed the way to Baitadi and said the village of Bangsalla was only a half hour's walk. Perhaps here I would find somewhere to get dry. But to my dismay Bangsalla was a Brahmin village, and I was politely but firmly shown the way out.

The Baitadi path wound up and down through rice paddies, and time and again I lost it for a well-trodden field track which would end up in somebody's back garden. I spent the day tripping over chickens, apologising to breastfeeding mothers, explaining how much my wretched boots cost and begging please, oh please, could you put me back on the right path. If I was curtly received now it was not, I suspect, to do with my caste so much as the glint of desperation in my eye. I could easily have been mistaken for a convict – if such people exist in Nepal. At any rate I was always hustled quickly back on to the proper path, and like a clockwork train I would shoot away, only to come off again a few hundred yards further on.

I slept in a tumbledown shed, which tumbled down a little more during the night as a result of a minor earthquake. I missed the main tremor, but awoke to find myself covered in dust. Too exhausted to be really frightened, I managed to drag myself outside and sat shivering on the path. The countryside around me seemed to be holding its breath – a thousand creatures waiting, like me, for something to happen. Some birds twittered nervously in the bamboo. At least they seemed satisfied that it was a false alarm, and settled down to sleep. I waited another ten minutes, then took my cue and did the same. Does this sound blasé? I hope not. No one can live through an earthquake, however small, without feeling some sort of terror. But my strength, if you can call it that, came from the fact that by this stage my reactions were so laggardly that by the time I fully realised what was happening, it was over.

By now there were clear signs that I was nearing the end. Along the path, Indo-Aryan faces had completely replaced Mongoloid ones. Occasionally a sari would make a splash of bright colour against the mountainside. Shops appeared along the way, their dimly lit shelves displaying Indian tobacco and biscuits. When porters asked where I was going, I would reply now 'India-maa jaanchhu – I'm going to India', and they would nod solemnly, telling me how they too had often been to India, taking *ghiu* (clarified butter) for export and bringing Indian wares back to Nepal.

Without warning, I rounded a bluff and laid eyes on the frontier. And what a frontier! The Mahakali had carved a gorge 4,000 feet deep, splitting the Himalaya and marking the end of the terraced hillsides and forested lekhs that make up Nepal's far west. Beyond lay the arid and barren hills of Almora, leading ultimately to Zanskar, Kashmir and the Karakoram. *Mahakali* means 'River of the Goddess Kali', but as *maha* also means honey, I preferred to think of it as the River of Honey.

I started the descent with mixed emotions. I was desperately undernourished and dirty, and my feet were truly on their last legs. But the rhythm of the walk, the pattern of effort involved in getting through each day, the slow but steady progress across mountains and valleys, had, like the dirt, got under my skin. I found myself slowing down even more, if that was possible, savouring the feeling of being within sight of my destination without actually being there. I dawdled in Baitadi itself, a delightful hilltop bazaar town where a Peace Corps volunteer had written 'Merry Christmas' in huge red letters across the front of her house. I stopped at every tea-house on the road. And still the twin riverside villages of Jhulaghat, and the old suspension bridge between them which would mark the end of the walk, drew closer. Mule trains made their way past me up the hill, with cargoes of kerosene and colourful Indian cloths. Their bells added a doleful ring to the familiar sounds of dogs and chickens in the farmyards.

On the upward draught from the gorge soared a pair of Himalayan griffons, the giant vultures that I had often seen from a distance, but never before close up. The nine foot wing-spans of these birds rivalled those of the condors that had accompanied me in the Andes – and which were, indeed, distant relatives. On the ground they were as ungainly as clockwork ducks, but now, in their own element, they were acrobats. Back and forth they soared effortlessly along the ridge, craning their scraggy necks to get a better look at me as they drifted by. After a quarter of an hour they tired of this game and turned south towards the Ganga plain. I'm sure I saw them dip their wings as they went on their way.

I hadn't seen the holy man approach. His footsteps had been light and his cloak was camouflaged with the dust of the road. He had come from the direction of the gorge – from India. Now he stood squarely in front of me, leaning on his stick, a wisp of a smile on his bearded face as he put his hands together in greeting. '*Namaste saathi.*'

We sat down together on a rock, and watched the griffons until they were specks in the distant haze. 'Fine birds,' he said in English. 'I sometimes wish I could travel like that.'

I looked at him in surprise. 'You speak English?'

'Of course.' He pointed to the west. 'I was born the son of a *sanyasin*, a Hindu priest, in Himachal Pradesh. But I learned English in Mussoorie – at the British school.' He saw my disbelief. 'Oh, there are many Indians there,' he reassured me. 'Or were. It was a long time ago.'

We introduced ourselves and shared some roasted corn. B. L. Parwana ('Call me B.L.') was a *sadhu*, a Hindu ascetic who after a successful business career in Chandigarh had left the comforts of his home and family to cultivate more spiritual disciplines. In the words of his religion, he had denounced the Path of Desire and entered the last of the four stages of life: the Path of Renunciation. The great Hindu scripture known as the *Laws of Manu* advises that when a man sees wrinkles on his face and grey hairs on his head, and when his sons are themselves fathers of sons, then he should 'betake himself to the forest'. Wearing a single garment and carrying only a staff and a begging bowl, he should spend his remaining years as a pilgrim, not soliciting provender or shelter but surviving on whatever may be freely offered along the way. Often he may find he can help his benefactors in return, by sharing his wisdom, but his primary purpose in this journey is to unite aatmaa with brahma, the soul with the universe, and so find a meaning in life beyond worldly things.

B.L. – an exemplary traveller, an explorer *par excellence*, a man more accomplished in both hedonistic and spiritual worlds than I would ever be – took a keener interest in my walk than anybody else I had met. He quizzed me on my reasons for doing it, my earlier aspirations and my feelings now; he commiserated with my injuries; he inquired about the state of the paths. Then abruptly he stood up and rummaged in his shoulder bag. 'Come, John-ji, we must make pujaa. You say your journey is nearly over, but I think it is just about to begin. We must make sure you have Shiva on your side.'

Shiva: the Destroyer. The god who presides over the deaths of worn-out spirits and their transformation into new ones. The divine alchemist of the Hindus. Of course! To B.L. it would be second nature to make a gesture to Shiva at the conclusion of any important task. But how peculiar that he should talk not about this task that was almost over, but about another one not yet started. As he daubed my forehead with the crimson tika powder that signified Shiva's approval, we talked further and I began to understand what he was trying to say. The walk, with its good days and bad days, its occasional sudden joys and innumerable wrong turnings, and towards the end its physical agonies, was no more than a preparation for travels still to come. It had given me a fore-taste of possible future journeys, not all necessarily geo-graphical ones. It was on these that I would need Shiva by my side.

From across the Mahakali came a drone. A truck was crawling up the opposite side of the gorge. It was the first motor vehicle I had seen or heard in more than two months. The new journey had begun.

Like a magician B.L. produced two fresh marigolds, though I had seen none growing nearby. He put them ceremoniously in my hair. Then he picked up his shoulder bag and stick and turned to go. 'Wait a minute,' I said, delving frantically into my pocket for some rupees. 'You haven't told me about your journey yet.'

B.L. smiled, took the money and gave a small dignified bow. 'My journey is like your next one will be. Endless. At the moment I'm making a little pilgrimage to the Festival of Shivaratri at Pashupatinath. It's more or less where you've just come from – near Kathmandu.'

A thought seemed to strike him. 'I don't suppose you'd like to sell me your boots?'

9

Return

'It was but yesterday we met in a dream.

You have sung to me in my aloneness, and I of your longings have built a tower in the sky.

But now our sleep has fled and our dream is over, and it is no longer dawn.

The noontide is upon us and our half waking has turned to a fuller day, and we must part.

If in the twilight of memory we should meet once more, we shall speak again together and you shall sing to me a deeper song.

And if our hands should meet in another dream we shall build another tower in the sky.'

Kahlil Gibran, *The Prophet*

It doesn't do to approach immigration officers with flowers in your hair – especially if you want to enter their country at a place that's supposed to be restricted to nationals only. They were waiting for me at the end of the bridge, faded khaki uniforms hiding pot bellies. I received a stern look, a salute and an invitation to sit down. They examined my passport page by page, even the blank ones. At length the man in charge asked in Nepali where I had come from and where in India I thought I might be going.

I took note of the 'thought'. 'I've come from Pokhara,' I said as brightly as possible. 'And I'd like to go somewhere where I can find a way of getting back to Kathmandu. Preferably without using my feet.'

The officer raised his eyebrows and spoke very slowly in English. 'And where, exactly, is this "Pokhara"?'

'Oh, it's over there.' I waved nervously towards what I hoped was Nepal – in the gorge it was difficult to tell. A frown swept across his face. 'A long way over there,' I added.

The officer looked doubtful. He looked as his assistants, whose eyes had been wandering towards my boots. They jerked to attention and looked dutifully doubtful too.

At length he spoke again. 'Your passport seems to be in order but I cannot let you into India. This crossing point is for Indian and Nepalese citizens only. If I let you through I would have to put an entry stamp in your passport.' He hesitated, examining his fingernails theatrically. 'Of course, I might be able to oblige ... ' I fished in my pocket. '... if I had an entry stamp ...' I took out twenty rupees. '... but I haven't.'

'Do you ever make exceptions?' I asked, toying with the twenty rupee note.

'Not in the ten years I've been on this job,' he replied. 'To tell the truth, we've never had any aliens here before.'

He looked at the twenty rupee note, then at the marigolds in my hair. There was an awkward silence. I rummaged in my

143

pocket and found another ten rupees. He seemed to decide. 'Of course,' he said, 'if you were not going to be staying in India ...'

'Only long enough to get back to Kathmandu.'

'... more than a few days, then I could say you were in transit.'

'That sounds just what I am.' I tentatively held out the money. 'Port tax?'

'Thirty rupees exactly.' He broke into a broad smile and accepted the notes. 'Now, would you like to join us in a cup of tea?'

The twin villages of Jhulaghat had one thing in common: they were filthy. Like many border communities, they seemed to have attracted the scum of both countries. On the Nepalese side the alleyways were ankle deep in mud, which had combined with the detritus of the customs inspection office – abandoned packaging, mangled metal and rotting fruit – to produce a lethal mixture underfoot. On the Indian side the streets were wider and it was easier to see where you were putting your feet. This was due in no small part to the electric lights which had recently been installed, and which seemed to be as much of a novelty to the inhabitants as they were to me. People nodded gravely when I pointed to the flickering bulbs, the first I had seen since Pokhara. After weeks of living with only the sun and moon for illumination I was mesmerised by them; I could have watched them blinking for hours. The people of Jhulaghat must have shared my awe, because many of them, open-mouthed, were doing just that. For once I understood how things that in Europe we take for granted are transforming the lives of people in remote places all over the world, just as they did for our grandparents in years gone by. It occurred to me too that the path to the new technology is not always a smooth one. In Jhulaghat they hadn't any switches yet, so the bulbs were left on night and day until they expired.

I was sitting on a wall, staring absent-mindedly at one of these miraculous light bulbs, when I noticed a crowd gathering across the street. It was only a small crowd, even for Jhulaghat, but nothing much else was happening so I went across to join them. Attention was centred on a bearded Hindu clutching a battered box. He placed it carefully on the ground, opened the lid, took out a wooden flute and began to play. He played well; under the pulsating light bulbs, the music was hypnotic. After a few minutes something stirred in the box. I craned forward to see and quickly craned back again. Out of the box rose a black snake, writhing its body and shaking its head from side to side as if to say 'No, no, no!' – like the immigration man at the bridge. This unusual busker earned a round of applause for his brief act, and collected a few coins before picking up the box with its snake and sauntering contentedly off. For me, he redeemed Jhulaghat completely. For all its squalor, any place these days that could still support a snake charmer couldn't be that bad.

The walk was over, but I still had a lot of travelling to do. To return to Kathmandu I would first have to go south across the hills of Almora to the Ganga plain, then re-enter Nepal at its south-western tip and make my way via Mahendranagar to Dhangadhi where there was an airstrip. From there I might, some said, be able to get a flight to Kathmandu. Failing this I would have to go back to India, because even from that relatively important part of Nepal there was still no road out.

I was in luck. A bus was due to depart the next morning for Pithoragarh, a town twenty miles from Jhulaghat in the hills to the west. As usual, the timetable said it would leave at 6 am. As usual, it left at 7.30. The higher slopes of the gorge had already shed their morning mist and were bathed in winter sunshine as the bus ground its way up the zigzag road. With my gloves I cleared the frost from its cracked window and peered out.

Gradually, as the miles crept by, it dawned on me why aliens were not welcome in this part of Uttar Pradesh. Grim-faced Indian soldiers were marching along the road, their faces coated with dust whipped up by convoys of camouflaged trucks. Barbed wire bristled in the fields. Finally, an hour from Jhulaghat, we arrived at a new and hideous military base,

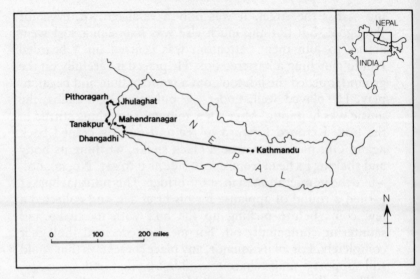

8 Return to Kathmandu

quite the most lavishly equipped I have ever seen. To my horror the road passed right through the middle. From the frenzied activity all around one could have been forgiven for thinking that the country was preparing for an imminent invasion, and indeed for all I knew it might have been. Resigning myself to almost certain arrest and detention, I lay low in my seat and waited for the inevitable. At least in my dishevelled state I felt fitting for the part, a worthiness dramatically enhanced by some dark glasses I had acquired in Jhulaghat. But to my chagrin nobody took the slightest notice of this impromptu impersonation of a spy. The bus rattled through the base and, as if to crown the insult, stopped shortly afterwards at a tourist guest house where breakfast was being served.

Pithoragarh was a sand-blown town set in arid, uninspiring hills. I changed buses and turned south. For seven hours the second bus bounced and shuddered along a road sometimes no wider than the paths I had been following in Nepal. Passengers clung to the roof-rack and fenders as we climbed two passes and crossed two more great river valleys, before descending to the foothills and finally to the plain. When I alighted at Tanakpur I found myself just two miles from the same Mahakali River that I had set out from that morning.

The river, which at Jhulaghat had been surging between rocky cliffs less than a hundred feet apart, was now a mile wide, dividing and rejoining languidly around gravel bars. It was spanned by the steel and concrete sluices of an Indian flood control barrage, the road back to Nepal a mere strip of tarmac clinging to its massive girders. Surrounded by bicycles, rickshaws and spluttering scooters, I had another tussle with the Indian immigration men, who asked again and again how I could possibly want to leave the country when according to my passport I had never entered it. This, it emerged, was a joke, but I was too tired and hungry to see it. I said I was in transit. They laughed. All jokers now, we drank the obligatory cup of tea, and after what seemed like an age I was at last back in Nepal and walking down the road to Mahendranagar.

In the failing light a jeep passed, anointed me with dust and lurched to a stop. A chubby Nepalese face grinned out from behind the steering wheel. 'Hello,' it said in English. 'Are you going my way?'

Now there is only one road in the whole of west Nepal, and we were on it. I examined the chubby face, trying to make out if this was another joke. 'Well,' I hesitated, 'I *was* thinking of going to Mahendranagar.'

'What luck,' said the chubby face without a hint of irony. 'So am I. Hop in.'

We bounced on. The ruts were dreadful, quite the worst I have ever experienced. Where the bridges were supposed to be we dived down into sandy river-beds which the jeep negotiated at perilous angles, half underwater, like those advertisements for Range Rovers. The chubby man drove casually, almost flippantly, as if he did this every day. After two abortive attempts in the bouncing cab he found my hand and shook it. 'Binod Bisht's the name. Pleased to meet you. Would you like to come back to my place? We've got a spare bed, you can stay the night, and tomorrow if you like you can come and watch the National Kabbadi Championships.'

It was an offer I couldn't refuse. Yes, I said, ducking to avoid going through the roof; I'd be delighted to. I spent the rest of the journey wondering what kabbadi was. After twenty minutes we turned off the road, if you could call it that, and pulled up by a thatched timber cottage outside which a log fire blazed. Around the flames half a dozen men were warming themselves in the chilly evening air, squatting easily on their haunches. They rose at our approach and sauntered over.

Binod, it seemed, was in the timber business. He also had what he called a modest interest in the building trade: a logical sideline since it provided him with a ready market for his timber products, and, unlike many building contractors in Nepal, he never ran out of materials. In addition to all this, he was chairman of the National Kabbadi Championships' organising committee.

In case, like me, you were wondering, kabbadi is like rugby without the ball. It is popular all over the Indian subcontinent, but in Nepal it is a national obsession. Teams of seven face each other across a field about a quarter the size of a football pitch. One man from one team crosses the centre line, muttering 'Kabbadi, kabbadi, kabbadi' as if it were a curse. His aim is to tag a member of the opposing team and then return to his own half. The other team bobs and sidesteps to avoid him, and if he does succeed in touching one the rest immediately rush at him shouting '*Grrrr!*', bringing him down, if they can, in a kind of rugby tackle. The best players dodge this attack and get back to their own side unscathed, still muttering 'Kabbadi, kabbadi, kabbadi' – because one of the rules is that you mustn't pause for breath.

The morning after I arrived, in a field on the edge of Mahendranagar, fourteen teams faced each other in the national championships – one from each of Nepal's fourteen zones. The crowd was at fever pitch; honour was at stake. Penalties were awarded for foul play, and everyone cheered or booed accordingly. In this small field in the south-western corner of Nepal, the excitement was every bit as intense as if we were watching the Olympic Games themselves. The sportsmanship was superb; linesmen's decisions were accepted without question. And when the winners marched up to receive their trophy from the Minister for Sport, the other teams gave them such a rousing ovation that the Minister's speech was completely drowned.

But back to Binod Bisht, or to be more precise, to his equally chubby young brother Anup, in whose delightful thatched cottage I had been found a bed. Anup was the playboy of the family, a frequent visitor to Kathmandu, from which he would return with assorted electronic bric-à-brac, an empty wallet and the sad sexual frustrations of a soft porn addict. Anup, poor man, was a devout Hindu. He worshipped with his family and played his part in all the rituals of his religion. But like so many people in traditional cultures, he had had a glimpse of what he fondly believed to be the Western way of life – and fancied what he saw. Of course, it was mostly a myth, a stereotyped series of images put across by advertisements and films; but it was tearing Anup apart. He listened thoughtfully when I described how many of us in the West, far from living the lives he dreamed of, were actually trying to establish equal opportunities, equal responsibilities and equal dignity for men and women. He said he thoroughly approved of this, and hoped that one day the same ideas would be accepted in Nepal. Then in the next breath he apologised that he hadn't been able to find me a girl for the night.

In practice, many Nepalese do have quite a liberal attitude towards sex. Marriage by no means puts an end to casual affairs, especially when husbands are away for long periods, either up in the higher grazing grounds or, in the case of the Sherpas, in the employment of a trekking agency or mountaineering expedition. Fair-skinned people are considered to be the most desirable, but the average Nepalese seems to have little idea of what makes for mutual attraction between men and women. An individual is more likely to rely on charms or spells to woo his partner than on any specific efforts of his own – a recourse also considered efficacious when cattle refuse to mate. Unfortunately I think it will be many years before women are permitted to take the same initiatives as men. Revealingly, Anup's mother and sister cooked all our meals while I was there, yet were never once allowed to come and meet me; they sent the meals across to the cottage with a servant. For Anup, I think eventually his faith will be the dominant influence in his life, and he will marry the girl chosen by his parents, and she will have half a dozen children and do all the cooking and housework. But I suspect he will still make clandestine visits to the nightspots of Kathmandu, and harbour a secret desire to live the wild, uninhibited life that he will always believe lies somewhere over the western horizon. At least Anup will have another life to fall back on in this faraway pocket of Nepal. Thousands of others, mostly in great cities like Singapore, Bangkok and Hong Kong, have sold their souls to the myth and have nowhere else to go.

Describing a visit to this area in 1967, the Nepalese author Harka Gurung wrote:

> We walked eastwards to Mahendranagar along a forest path under tall sal trees festooned with giant creepers, and wove our way past large anthills. Mahendranagar, about 270 metres above sea level, was a new settlement in the middle of the forest with the foothills visible to the north.

Sixteen years later I found the trees had all gone. Settlers from the hills had cleared most of them to plant crops, and timber companies like Binod's had seen to the rest. The forest path had been replaced by the road along which I had bounced in Binod's jeep – the first stage of a highway that would eventually link Mahendranagar with Kathmandu. Yet this was the very spot where in 1876 the Rana prime minister Jang Bahadur had taken the Prince of Wales (later Edward VII) hunting for big forest game. The royal party, transported through the woods and swamps by an army of 800 elephants, had on that occasion bagged a leopard, twenty Bengal tigers and no less than a hundred deer. Now, staring across the open plain, the only things I could see piercing the horizon were telegraph poles, and the only wildlife some scruffy mynah birds perched on the wires.

I was still having trouble with my knees, so was in hardly any state to resist the brothers' pampering. Quite the opposite in fact: I loved it. By day I would take a rickshaw into Mahendranagar, now a city of 5,000 people, and gape at the goods in the shops; or I would limp across to Binod's sawmill and watch the last remaining trees of south-west Nepal being sliced up like loaves of bread. By night I would lie back and watch the stars drift across the sky, dreaming of leopards and Bengal tigers. In spite of Anup's concern about the lack of female company, we spent some entertaining evenings round his ample campfire, one of the perks of having a brother in the timber trade. Anup revealed himself to be an accomplished bongoist, and the brothers and I would sing old Cat Stevens songs (the only ones, it turned out, that we all knew the words to) until the moon rose high in the sky and we only just had enough energy to stumble off sleepily to our beds. Anup's and Binod's hospitality was boundless: exactly what the doctor would have ordered for me, if there had been one within fifty miles.

Eventually, reluctantly, I took my leave of them. In the clinging early morning mist I flagged down the bus that rattled its way daily towards the airstrip at Dhangadhi. It was a thirty-five mile journey which, because of the innumerable bridges that hadn't been built yet, was scheduled to take four hours. It took six. The road deteriorated until it was no more than a string of joined-up potholes. We never exceeded ten miles per hour, yet were jolted and jarred until I was sure my limbs would part company with my body. A seat sheared off its mountings and crashed against the side of the bus. The driver shrugged. Why worry? Nobody had been sitting on it.

This road, whose eastern section I had used four months previously to reach Kathmandu, will when completed be the key to the future of Nepal. (Hopefully they will have filled in some of the potholes by then.) It is being built in stages across

151

the northern rim of the Ganga plain – the 'Terai' to the Nepalese – a 620 mile ribbon linking east and west. The project makes good economic sense. Although the Kathmandu valley is Nepal's political and cultural centre, it is the Terai, with its rich soils and subtropical climate, which is the centre of food production. Occupying less than a quarter of the country, the Terai produces more than three-quarters of its national harvest, especially when it comes to those crops that prefer low altitudes, like rice and maize. It is rightly known as the grain basket of Nepal. Until recent times the whole area was infested with malaria and inhabited only by a handful of Tharu people who had somehow developed immunity from this killer disease. As malaria was progressively eradicated in the 1950s and 1960s, however, people came down from the hills and began to exploit the fertile soil. At first the Terai was seen merely as a refuge in times of famine, but today it is the target of permanent resettlement on a grand scale, encouraged (and often directed) by the government. It was to the Terai that the people of RaRa came when they were thrown out of their village to make way for the national park; here also ended up many of the refugees from the far western hills after their villages were lost in the 1966 earthquake.

At first, the settlers simply cleared patches in the sal forest wherever the land seemed easiest to work. They prospered, and word of their fortune spread. Between 1970 and 1980 the Terai's population doubled, so that today it is the forest which forms patches in a landscape dominated by paddy-fields, dirt roads and seemingly endless lines of creaky carts drawn by bullocks, oxen or pouting water buffalo. It must be admitted that the deforestation here has served a purpose. Although the leopards are all but gone and the Bengal tigers and deer are limited to just four reserves, the destruction has enabled a great many Nepalese to lift themselves out of the poverty which used to hamper their lives in the mountains – an existence forever from hand to mouth, where they depended on good harvests for their very survival. In contrast to the deforestation of the high valleys, which is a doomed effort to

152

exploit a dwindling resource, the old regime in the Terai is being replaced by a new, productive and valuable one.

In Dhangadhi I went to the airline office and immediately wished I hadn't. The plane from Kathmandu, which usually came daily, had been unable to get through for ten days because of bad weather in the mountains. The clerk put my name at the bottom of what looked like a very long waiting list. I took a rickshaw through sugar-cane and swamp to the airstrip and settled down to wait.

There were several others in the waiting room, in various stages of slumber: plump government officials, a couple of skinny European volunteer workers and a smartly dressed American with a twitch. After an hour or so a Nepalese in army uniform emerged from an office, introduced himself as the airport manager (rather grandly, I thought, as he seemed to be the only person there) and said he had received a radio message that the flight had left Nepalganj and was heading our way. The other passengers were unimpressed by this news; they had heard it all before. Nevertheless, half an hour later there did appear a speck in the eastern sky. The government officials pointed and began to stir, followed drowsily by the rest. The speck grew larger, transformed itself into a de Havilland Twin Otter, circled once and landed with a cough.

Unbelievably, there was room for us all. I found myself sitting next to the man with the twitch, who introduced himself as Wilbur.

Wilbur was no sightseer. He offered me his window seat and buried himself in the contents of his briefcase, as for two and a half hours I watched two and a half months of walking slip under the wing. The Karnali, the Bheri, the Uttar Ganga went by. In the enthusiasm of the moment I gripped Wilbur's elbow and pointed to the gorge where I had almost fallen off the ledge. He peered through the porthole at the scene of my near demise. 'I've just come from there,' he said at last. 'It's been shortlisted for a dam.'

Kathmandu, Lucknow, Delhi, London – buses, trains, more planes. Although my spirit remained in Nepal, the rest of me was homeward bound. Mercifully the impersonal and almost indecent fervour which besets travel in the West did not sully my railway journey across India. I had the delight of two days sharing a compartment with a sitarist, an irrepressible raconteur and an army officer with a shaved head and no teeth. Our earnest discussions echoed forth upon the winds of Uttar Pradesh, and as usual I understood hardly a word. But every time I nodded, whether in agreement or somnolence, the raconteur shook me vigorously by the hand and the army officer slapped his thigh, repeating emphatically whatever had just been said, as best he could without his teeth. I ended up at midnight following these three crackpots down the tracks, after our train had stopped half a mile short of Mathura, apparently out of steam. We nearly got killed when it changed its mind and came thundering down the line after us.

At Delhi I had already left the East behind. The city which six months earlier had so fascinated my innocent eyes now seemed prosperous and dull. Rashtrapati Bhavan, the Red Fort, even the magnificent mosque of Jama Masjid were like so many tourist attractions – pompous and meaningless. My mind was still in the mountains as my body found its way through the brightly lit night streets towards the airport and home.

Some weeks later the same body was looking across English water meadows – the ones where the previous year I had strolled up and down the riverside footpaths going over the case for my trip. It was March now, and the pale days of the European winter were beginning to give way to the stronger light of spring. The morning frost had quickly disappeared; there was warmth in the soil. A thin mist rose from the river, drifted in the hint of a breeze and dispersed among the willows on the opposite bank. At the water's edge fragile shoots were already visible: a promise of the meadowsweet, marsh marigold and loosestrife which would come with full summer. The mallard of my previous visit had gone, but a pair of pochard ducks had made the river their winter home and were bustling about among the coots and moorhens, quacking broodily as they collected material for their nest. The valley was coming out of hibernation; the subdued hues and muted calls of winter were making way for richer colours and sounds.

Along with these changes I was aware of some fundamental changes in me. The trip had made me rethink some cherished ideas. First and most ill-informed of these was that Eastern philosophies were somehow not applicable to the Western condition; that having their origins in mysticism rather than pragmatism, they would somehow fail when it came to dealing with practical problems. I could not have been more wrong. Some of the ways of thinking I came across in Nepal were far in advance of any we have developed in the West. Buddhists, for example, by emphasising the importance of change, draw attention to how transient everything is and are constantly mindful of the dangers of attachment, especially to living things. The meditant at RaRa Tal, who had a good sense of humour, had laughed at himself as he explained this to me. But I think he was also smiling at the lunacy of our Western preoccupation with *things* rather than the circumstances which give us these things, and which will ultimately, inevitably, take them away again. Sixty years ago the Indian philosopher Sarvepalli Radhakrishnan wrote:

How do we come to think of things, rather than of processes in this absolute flux? By shutting our eyes to the successive events. It is an artificial attitude that makes sections in the stream of change, and calls them things ... When we shall know the truth of things, we shall realise how absurd it is for us to worship isolated products of the incessant series of transformations as though they were eternal and real. Life is no thing or state of a thing, but a continuous movement or change.

The importance of this message (and that of my friend B.L. too) only came to me when I began to look from this new

155

perspective at my second long-cherished idea. I had gone to Nepal clutching some common Western afflictions – insecurities, broken romances, lost dreams – and had had a vague notion that the trip would somehow wipe the slate clean: would lay the foundations for a fresh start. If I learned one thing in Nepal it was that life is not about wiping slates clean and making fresh starts. The painful experiences we go through, agonising and unfair though they may seem, are the rocks in the sand on which we build our characters. Far from being catastrophes they are absolutely essential to our growing up. They are the clifftop ledges and icy streams of our journey, which give it substance and meaning and which prepare us for more difficult journeys in future.

The Buddhist of RaRa Tal and the Hindu, B.L., were in their own fashions both gently propelling me towards the same conclusion: that life is not about ends and goals, but about the changes that happen along the way. What they were saying was hardly new. Confucian philosophers, approaching the question centuries earlier, had taken almost exactly the same standpoint in the Book of Changes, the *I Ching*. So had Einstein when he first put forward relativity theory. And so, curiously enough, had the school of scientists who challenged Einstein and founded the later versions of quantum theory.

These wise people all looked from their different points of view at a world of uncertainty and saw changes. Blossoming and withering, enrichment and impoverishment, expansion and contraction, growth and decay. Gradual changes, sudden changes. Changes for the better, changes for the worse. They differed widely in their interpretation of the changes they saw, but they seem to have agreed on one thing: people generally don't like change. I would go further and say that many people *hate* change. I should like to go into this a little more deeply because I think it was the most important thing I learned in Nepal.

People hate change for the very good reason that most changes are painful. The change from childhood to adulthood involves the pain of giving up one's innocence; the change from adulthood to old age brings on the pain of inadequacy and decay. Even changes that open up great opportunities often arouse the pain of insecurity and the fear of challenge. Given the choice, therefore, many people will avoid the risk of pain by keeping things as much as possible as they are.

The Buddha recognised this paramount importance of pain in determining what we do. He embodied it in the first of his four 'Noble Truths' which may be roughly translated as *life is suffering*. In the Buddha's view, suffering came from grasping for things one could not have, and holding on to things when one ought to let them go. 'All things arise and pass away,' he declared. As long as people tried to resist the irresistible changes in and around them, they would always suffer.

The other three 'Noble Truths' were concerned with how to escape from the vicious circle. Essentially, once one accepts change and pain as positive things – the seeds from which one grows and without which one cannot grow – much of the pain will disappear of its own accord. This is not to suggest that when threatened one should stand idly by. On the contrary, some of the greatest improvements to the world have come about through people's reactions to adversity. All he meant to stress was the importance of living in the present – warts and all.

Considering the pitfalls of some of our journeys through life, most people start out with a rotten map. For one thing many of its features are drawn up during childhood on the basis of information from grown-ups, which means that it is full of distortions and inaccuracies and out of date from the beginning. Like my map of west Nepal, such a mental map of the world will lead one up innumerable blind alleys and may prove so frustrating that one is tempted to give up the journey altogether. Luckily one can make changes to these maps as one goes along. Once I had discovered that the Dhole Khola went south instead of west, I put this on my tatty dyeline print and immediately felt more confident. Most people have learned how to revise their mental maps of the world pretty well as they go through life. If they do stray up an unmarked cul-de-sac, they plot it clearly so they won't make the same mistake again. The main difficulty people seem to have with their maps is when it comes to changes that happen to things they thought they knew.

Roads, paths, bridges, villages, even rivers and mountains come and go. If you don't update your map, you may walk over a precipice. Yet we all know people who persistently live in the past, going around with obsolete maps in their heads even when reality is staring them in the face. If the changes they see look painful they simply ignore them. It is amazing how many people actually choose to abandon their journey altogether, and stay wherever they happen to be, rather than give up the cherished misconceptions which make up their mental map. They reach the unmarked landslide, and instead of scrambling round it they simply stand looking at it for the rest of their lives. I know. I nearly did myself.

Whatever the similarities, our mental maps will always be different in one respect from 'real' maps, like mine of west Nepal. Reality in Nepal was easy to define; the map was either right or wrong. (Mostly it was wrong.) Reality in terms of life's journey is not such a simple matter. It comes in various versions. A Hindu's version is different from a Buddhist's, for example, because he puts a different interpretation on things. So is a Navajo Indian's from an Eskimo's, an ice-cream salesman's from a heating engineer's, yours from mine. Even people with similar versions of reality will tend to emphasise different aspects on their mental maps: easy routes, danger areas, beauty spots. The only test of a map in the face of all these possible variations is whether it gets you where you want to go.

I think people are content to put up with bad maps because they often make the journey seem easier than it really is. Show all the mountains and the way ahead looks pretty formidable; omit one or two and, my goodness, you're nearly there. Dedication to the truth is difficult when the truth is awful. Most of us avoid it when we can. We kid ourselves into thinking that our preferred version of the map is the true one: that the mountains are genuinely not there.

But as with changes, if accepting the truth is painful, then not accepting it is almost certain to be more painful still.

I'm sure the reason why the truth is often so painful is that it requires us to give up so much. The meditant's message at RaRa Tal was that I should perhaps give up some of the goals I had set for the walk – or at least not be so obsessive about them. B.L.'s advice was similar: give up your preoccupation with beginnings and ends, and concentrate on what goes on in between. Giving up things is certainly not something I find easy. (You probably noticed I didn't actually follow the advice of either of them.) It is an acquired talent. Giving up food, sex and material things, I can just about manage; giving up opinions, ideas, attitudes and ambitions, I'm working on; and I suppose one day, like everyone, I'll have to face the prospect of giving up my life. But isn't this the nub of what B.L. was trying to tell me: that the end of these dear things would simply be the beginning of something else? And that far from being impoverished if I let them go, I would grow as a result, and through my growth become richer?

I think B.L. had put his finger on a profound truth. His reasoning not only made sense of the pain we experience, by showing that only through suffering can we grow. But it also provided a clue to a closely related question that has been occupying philosophers' minds since time began: the question of love.

I would define 'love' as the will and ability to help someone grow in the way that suits him or her best. This would apply equally to loving others or loving yourself. It is a useful definition because it helps explain what is perhaps the most basic truth of all: love hurts. If, to grow, you have to give up ideas that you have fondly held since childhood, it hurts. If, to grow, someone you love has to give up things you are fond of in them, it hurts. If, for someone you love to grow, you have to give up something – possibly even the actual loved one – again it hurts. Accepting the importance of giving up, however much it may hurt, is the key to love just as it is the key to growth.

'*The love you take is equal to the love you make,*' sang the

Beatles. I think they were wrong. You receive *more* love than you give. In spite of all this giving up and letting go it always, like growth, leaves you richer. It is one of those rarest of things, a self-replenishing resource.

In their own strange ways, the meditant and B.L. were both clearly showing a kind of love for me. I didn't realise it at the time, partly because I was still suffering from the Western delusion that one can't love a stranger, and partly because they both took me completely by surprise. I have wondered since whether I was in fact such a stranger to them after all. The meditant in particular seemed to know a great deal about me, and I would have been quite prepared, in that ruined village under the full moon, to have believed in other forms of communication besides the established ones. But whether they had higher powers or just a capacity for astute observation, their motives were unmistakable: to help me set aside my prejudices and grow.

I remember how odd it seemed that they should be inspired to do this when in all probability they would never see me again. But on reflection I think I understand. Love relies no more on feedback from the recipient than sound requires a listening ear or light a watching eye. It doesn't depend in the slightest on the loved one actually being there; it varies not a jot with the loved one's behaviour (as any parent will tell you). It is concerned only for the loved one's best interests – whatever they may be. Looking back on those meetings in the mountains, I am no longer surprised at the two men's apparent clairvoyance; nor even that they were willing to help a stranger give up some of his treasured ideas. Only one thing remains a mystery, and that is, what inspired them to choose me?

By the time you read this, many of the people and things described in this book will have gone. I can't vouch for the meditant of RaRa Tal, but I do know that Jumla's kerosene streetlights are no more. A hydroelectric scheme brought power to Jumla in 1984 – the first in Karnali Zone – and overhead cables now frame the view from the bazaar. Jim Fulton has moved on to Nigeria, and the British Embassy in

Kathmandu is very much the poorer without him. I suspect that Jhulaghat's snake charmer has moved on too.

I fear that a great deal more of north-west Nepal will have been carried away down the Budi Ganga by now. Until steps are taken to halt the deforestation of Nepal's valleys, soil erosion including landslides will be a feature of every monsoon. In the Solu-Khumbu district south of Mount Everest an effort is being made, with some success, to replant the worst affected areas with specially grown saplings. This may stall the crisis, but it will not resolve it because it is not tackling the cause of the problem which is an ever increasing demand for fodder and fuel. The highly efficient wood-burning stoves developed by Intermediate Technology offer more promise. In the villages where they have been introduced, they have helped to eliminate one of the causes of deforestation by cutting fuel requirements by half.

The Kolti airstrip is open and functioning, serving a wide area of the mid-Karnali and upper Budi Ganga valleys which previously could only be reached by many days' walking over difficult terrain. The Uttar Ganga, along with several other spectacular rivers, is still shortlisted for a dam.

Nepal is being dragged by its bootstraps into the twentieth century. I was lucky enough to observe this in a part of the country where the process is only just beginning, and I must say that I think some of the changes are not in the best interests of the Nepalese. But that is a Western view. The Nepalese have made it clear, by their actions as well as their words, that they welcome many of the changes that have happened and wish them to continue. The West has provided them for the first time in their history with a choice of paths, and in some cases – like an overbearing parent – has made the choice for them. The East, on the other hand, has given them extraordinary insight and an inner calm with which to face the changes and the pressures they bring. Those of us from the West who have been privileged to meet the Nepalese at home in their astonishing country remember them with well-deserved affection, expressed eloquently earlier this century by Sir Ralph Turner:

As I write these last words, my thoughts return to you who were my comrades, the stubborn and indomitable peasants of Nepal. Once more I hear the laughter with which you greeted every hardship ... Bravest of the brave, most generous of the generous, never had a country more faithful friends than you.

If, beyond affection, we claim also to *love* the Nepalese, we must allow them to grow and change in the way that suits them best.

Epilogue

Fordwells, Oxfordshire
14 June 1983

Dear John,

Your Christmas letter from Jumla has just reached us –
almost exactly six months late. We were so pleased to hear
from you; we thought you'd vanished into thin air. Merry
Christmas!

Beany

Glossary of Nepali words used in the text

Aamaa	mother
Aatmaa	soul
Aaunu	to come
Ah	yes ⎤ (in certain parts of
Aha	no ⎦ Nepal)
Baabu	father
Baas basnu	accommodation
Baato	road, way
Bhaat	boiled rice
Bhaati	tea-house, inn (literally 'rice-house')
Bhaau	value
Bhandaa	than
Bhut	demon
Brahma	(among Hindus) universe, god; specifically, the God of Creation
Chaltiko	popular, fashionable
Chang	home-made beer (usually from rice)
Chautaara	wayside resting place
Chha	there is, it is
Chhaina	there isn't, it isn't
Chilim	clay pipe (also called *tamakhu*)
Chini	sugar
Chorten	wayside shrine
Chuba	Tibetan cloak
Daal	lentils
– *Daal bhaat*	rice and lentils (the staple Nepalese dish)

164

Dekhi	from
Desh	country
– Mero desh	my country
– Tapaaiko desh	your country
Devanagari	Indian and Nepalese script
Dhairya	patience
Dharma	duty
Didi	(elder) sister
Doko	wicker basket
Dungaa	boat, canoe
Dzo	cross between a cow and a yak
Ekai	the same
Garnu	to do, to make
Ghat	riverside landing stage
Ghiu	clarified butter
Gompa	monastery
Goth	shepherd's hut
Haawaapaani	climate
Hajur	yes, 'sure'
Himal	mountain range
Ho	yes
Hoina	no
Hunu	to be
Jaanu	to go
-ji	suffix showing affection and respect
Kaaphar	coward
Kahaa?	where?
Kahaa jaane?	where are you going?
Khaanekuraa	food
Khola	river
Khukri	Nepalese curved knife
Kos	measure of distance (about two miles)
Kun?	which?

Lama	Buddhist priest
Lekh	range of hills (lower than *himal*)
-maa	to, in
Maachho	fish
Maake	maize flour
Maanaa	measure of weight (usually about 1 lb)
Maato	soil
Maha	honey
Mantra	incantation, prayer
Marnu	to die
Mithai	sweet, candy
Mohar	50 *paisaa* (about 2p sterling)
Murkha	stupid
Naamlo	tumpline for carrying *doko*
Naaur	wild blue sheep
Namaskaar	hello (formal) ⎫ with hands clasped
Namaste	hello (informal) ⎭ in greeting
Nirvana	(among Buddhists) awakening, heaven
Ohor-dohor	coming and going
– Ohar-dohor garne dungaa	'coming-and-going boat', ferry
Paainchha	there is available, it is available
Paani	water
– Taato	hot
– Tatopani, taatopaani	hot springs
Paisaa	one-hundredth of a rupee (also 'money' generally)
Panchayat	local council
Pani	also, too
Pujaa	Hindu ritual offering, usually of *tika*
Ra	and
Raamro	good, better
– Naraamro	bad, worse

Rakshi	spirit distilled from rice or barley
Roti	'bread' (usually chapatis)
Saarangi	Nepalese stringed instrument
Saathi	friend
Sadhu	Hindu ascetic, pilgrim
Sahib	sir
Sangu, saanghu	makeshift bridge
Sano, saano	small
Sanyasin	Hindu priest
Shaman	witch-doctor
Shiva	(among Hindus) the God of Destruction
Sukaa	25 *paisaa* (about 1p sterling)
Tal	lake
Tamakhu	clay pipe (also called *chilim*)
Tara	but
Tarkaari	green vegetables
Thik	right, correct, good
– *Thik chha*	that's good, all right, OK
Thulo	big, great
Tika	vermilion powder mixed with clay, used in Hindu rituals (see *pujaa*)
Topi	Nepalese hat
Tsampa	barley flour
Tyo	that
Yahaa	here
Yo	this
Yogi	meditant, monk

Bibliography

Several of these books have been published in more than one country. Original editions are quoted here, followed by British editions where they exist, but readers may find others available locally. For those published in Kathmandu the following suppliers are recommended:

Himalayan Booksellers
GPO Box 528
Gantaghar
Durbar Marg
Kathmandu

Ratna Pustak Bhandar
GPO Box 98
Bhotahity
Kathmandu

Places

Anderson, John Gottberg (ed.), *Nepal* (Hong Kong: Apa Productions; London: Harrap, 1983).

Bezruchka, Stephen, *A Guide to Trekking in Nepal* (Kathmandu: Sahayogi Prakashan, 1972; Leicester: Cordee; Seattle: The Mountaineers, 1981).

Gibbons, Bob, and Bob Ashford, *The Himalayan Kingdoms: Nepal, Bhutan and Sikkim* (London: Batsford, 1983).

Gurung, Harka, *Vignettes of Nepal* (Kathmandu: Sajha Prakashan, 1980).

Hagen, Toni, *Nepal: The Kingdom in the Himalayas* (Berne: Kümmerly & Frey, 1961; London: Robert Hale, 1972).

Herzog, Maurice (trans. Nea Morin and Janet Adam Smith), *Annapurna: Conquest of the First 8,000 Metre Peak* (London: Jonathan Cape, 1952).

Matthiessen, Peter, *The Snow Leopard* (New York: Viking Press, 1978; London: Chatto & Windus, 1979).

Morris, John, *A Winter in Nepal* (London: Hart-Davis, 1963).

Murphy, Dervla, *The Waiting Land: A Spell in Nepal* (London: John Murray, 1967).

Rowell, Galen, *Many People Come, Looking, Looking* (Seattle: The Mountaineers, 1980).

Snellgrove, David, *Himalayan Pilgrimage* (Boulder, Col.: Prajñā Press, 1981; Oxford: Bruno Cassirer, 1961).

Tilman, H. W., *Nepal Himalaya* (Cambridge: Cambridge University Press, 1952).

Tucci, Giuseppe (trans. Lovett Edwards), *Nepal: The Discovery of the Malla* (London: Allen & Unwin, 1962).

People

Anderson, Mary M., *The Festivals of Nepal* (London: Allen & Unwin, 1971).

Aziz, Barbara Nimri, *Tibetan Frontier Families* (New Delhi: Vikas, 1978).

Bista, Dor Bahadur, *People of Nepal* (Kathmandu: Ratna Pustak Bhandar, 1976).

Caplan A. Patricia, *Priests and Cobblers: A Study of Social Change in a Hindu Village in Western Nepal* (San Francisco: Chandler, 1972).

Ekvall, Robert B., *Fields on the Hoof* (New York: Holt, Rinehart & Winston, 1968).

Farwell, Byron, *The Gurkhas* (Harmondsworth: Allen Lane, 1984).

Fürer-Haimendorf, Christoph von, *Himalayan Traders* (London: John Murray, 1975).

Lall, Kesar, *Nepalese Customs and Manners* (Kathmandu: Ratna Pustak Bhandar, 1976).

Singh, Madanjeet, *Himalayan Art* (London: Macmillan, 1968).

Vaidya, Karunakar, *Folk Tales of Nepal* (Kathmandu: Ratna Pustak Bhandar, 1980).

Natural History

Fleming, Robert L. Sr., Robert L. Fleming Jr., and Lain S. Bangdel, *Birds of Nepal* (Kathmandu: Avalok, 1979).

Mishra, Hemant Raj, and Dorothy Mierow, *Wild Animals of Nepal* (Kathmandu: Ratna Pustak Bhandar, 1976).

Polunin, Oleg, and Adam Stainton, *Flowers of the Himalaya* (Oxford: Oxford University Press, 1985).

Schaller, George B., *Stones of Silence: Journeys in the Himalaya* (New York: Viking Press, 1980; London: André Deutsch, 1980).

Philosophy and Religion

Blofeld, John, *Beyond the Gods* (London: Allen & Unwin, 1974).

Buck, William (ed.), *Ramayana* (Berkeley: University of California Press, 1976).

Bühler, G. (trans.), *The Laws of Manu* (Sacred Books of the East, Vol. 25) (Oxford: Clarendon Press, 1886).

Capra, Fritjof, *The Turning Point* (New York: Simon & Schuster, 1982; London: Wildwood House, 1982).

Castaneda, Carlos, *The Teachings of Don Juan: A Yaqui Way of Knowledge* (Berkeley: University of California Press, 1968; Harmondsworth: Penguin, 1970).

Gibran, Kahlil, *The Prophet* (New York: Alfred A. Knopf, 1923; London: Heinemann/Pan, 1980).

Khantipalo, Bhikkhu, *Calm and Insight: A Buddhist Manual for Meditators* (London: Curzon Press, 1981).

Lao Tzu (trans. Ch'u Ta-Kao), *Tao Te Ching* (London: Allen & Unwin, 1972).

Narayan, R. K. (ed.), *The Mahabharata* (London: Heinemann, 1978).

Peck, M. Scott, *The Road Less Traveled* (New York: Simon & Schuster, 1978); published as *The Road Less Travelled* (London: Hutchinson, 1983).

Radhakrishnan, Sarvepalli, *Indian Philosophy*, 2 vols. (London: Allen & Unwin, 1923, 1927).

Rahula, Walpola, *What the Buddha Taught* (Bedford: Gordon Fraser, 1967).

Wilhelm, Richard (trans.), *The I Ching, or Book of Changes* (London: Routledge & Kegan Paul, 1968).

Zaehner, R. C., *Hinduism* (Oxford: Oxford University Press, 1962).

Other sources

Bloch, Arthur, *Murphy's Law* (Los Angeles: Price/Stern/Sloan, 1977; London: Magnum, 1979).

Davidson, Robyn, *Tracks* (London: Jonathan Cape, 1980).

Moorehead, Alan, *The White Nile* (London: Hamish Hamilton, 1960).

Peter, Laurence J., and Raymond Hull, *The Peter Principle* (New York: William Morrow, 1969; London: Souvenir Press, 1969).

Steinbeck, John, *Travels with Charley* (New York: Viking Press, 1962; London: Heinemann, 1962).

BIBLIOGRAPHY

Stevenson, Robert Louis, *Travels with a Donkey in the Cevennes* (London: Kegan Paul, 1879).

Turner, Sir Ralph, *A Comparative and Etymological Dictionary of the Nepali Language* (London: Kegan Paul, 1931).

Twain, Mark, *Following the Equator* (Hartford, Conn.: American Publishing Co., 1897); published as *More Tramps Abroad* (London: Chatto & Windus, 1897).